MznLnx

Missing Links Exam Preps

Exam Prep for

Nonprofit Marketing Best Practices

Burnett, 1st Edition

The MznLnx Exam Prep is your link from the texbook and lecture to your exams.
The MznLnx Exam Preps are unauthorized and comprehensive reviews of your textbooks.

All material provided by MznLnx and Rico Publications (c) 2010
Textbook publishers and textbook authors do not particpate in or contribute to these reviews.

MznLnx

Rico
Publications

Exam Prep for Nonprofit Marketing Best Practices
1st Edition
Burnett

Publisher: Raymond Houge
Assistant Editor: Michael Rouger
Text and Cover Designer: Lisa Buckner
Marketing Manager: Sara Swagger
Project Manager, Editorial Production: Jerry Emerson
Art Director: Vernon Lowerui

Product Manager: Dave Mason
Editorial Assitant: Rachel Guzmanji
Pedagogy: Debra Long
Cover Image: Jim Reed/Getty Images
Text and Cover Printer: City Printing, Inc.
Compositor: Media Mix, Inc.

(c) 2010 Rico Publications

ALL RIGHTS RESERVED. No part of this work covered by the copyright may be reproduced or used in any form or by an means--graphic, electronic, or mechanical, including photocopying, recording, taping, Web distribution, information storage, and retrieval systems, or in any other manner--without the written permission of the publisher.

Printed in the United States
ISBN:

For more information about our products, contact us at:
Dave.Mason@RicoPublications.com

For permission to use material from this text or product, submit a request online to:
Dave.Mason@RicoPublications.com

Contents

CHAPTER 1
Nonprofits: Yesterday, Today, and Tomorrow — 1

CHAPTER 2
The Essence of Marketing: Terms and Processes Nonprofits Need to Know — 5

CHAPTER 3
Approaching the Market — 17

CHAPTER 4
Marketing Research: The Foundation for Planning — 24

CHAPTER 5
External Considerations in Marketing Introduction — 31

CHAPTER 6
Transitioning to Services Marketing — 43

CHAPTER 7
Decision Making by Target Markets and Stakeholders — 48

CHAPTER 8
Creating and Managing Products — 56

CHAPTER 9
Communicating to Mass Markets — 68

CHAPTER 10
Pricing The Product — 75

CHAPTER 11
The Channels of Distribution — 82

CHAPTER 12
Raising Funds and Acquiring Volunteers — 86

ANSWER KEY — 91

TO THE STUDENT

COMPREHENSIVE

The *MznLnx* Exam Prep series is designed to help you pass your exams. Editors at MznLnx review your textbooks and then prepare these practice exams to help you master the textbook material. Unlike study guides, workbooks, and practice tests provided by the texbook publisher and textbook authors, *MznLnx* gives you **all** of the material in each chapter in exam form, not just samples, so you can be sure to nail your exam.

MECHANICAL

The MznLnx Exam Prep series creates exams that will help you learn the subject matter as well as test you on your understanding. Each question is designed to help you master the concept. Just working through the exams, you gain an understanding of the subject--its a simple mechanical process that produces success.

INTEGRATED STUDY GUIDE AND REVIEW

MznLnx is not just a set of exams designed to test you, its also a comprehensive review of the subject content. Each exam question is also a review of the concept, making sure that you will get the answer correct without having to go to other sources of material. You learn as you go! Its the easiest way to pass an exam.

HUMOR

Studying can be tedious and dry. MznLnx's instructional design includes moderate humor within the exam questions on occassion, to break the tedium and revitalize the brain

Chapter 1. Nonprofits: Yesterday, Today, and Tomorrow

1. _____ was a writer, management consultant, and self-described 'social ecologist.' Widely considered to be the father of 'modern management,' his 39 books and countless scholarly and popular articles explored how humans are organized across all sectors of society--in business, government and the nonprofit world. His writings have predicted many of the major developments of the late twentieth century, including privatization and decentralization; the rise of Japan to economic world power; the decisive importance of marketing; and the emergence of the information society with its necessity of lifelong learning. In 1959, Drucker coined the term 'knowledge worker' and later in his life considered knowledge work productivity to be the next frontier of management.
    a. Rick Boyce
    b. Peter Ferdinand Drucker
    c. Paschal Eze
    d. Nouveau riche

2. A _____ is a list of the general tasks and responsibilities of a position. Typically, it also includes to whom the position reports, specifications such as the qualifications needed by the person in the job, salary range for the position, etc. A _____ is usually developed by conducting a job analysis, which includes examining the tasks and sequences of tasks necessary to perform the job.
    a. Job description
    b. 6-3-5 Brainwriting
    c. Power III
    d. 180SearchAssistant

3. _____ is a term used to describe a person who was born during the demographic Post-World War II baby boom. Many analysts now believe that two distinct cultural generations were born during this baby boom; the older generation is often called the Baby Boom Generation and the younger generation is often called Generation Jones. The term '_____' is sometimes used in a cultural context, and sometimes used to describe someone who was born during the post-WWII baby boom.
    a. Greatest Generation
    b. Baby Boomer
    c. AStore
    d. Generation X

4. _____ is an advertisement in which a particular product specifically mentions a competitor by name for the express purpose of showing why the competitor is inferior to the product naming it.

This should not be confused with parody advertisements, where a fictional product is being advertised for the purpose of poking fun at the particular advertisement, nor should it be confused with the use of a coined brand name for the purpose of comparing the product without actually naming an actual competitor. ('Wikipedia tastes better and is less filling than the Encyclopedia Galactica.')

In the 1980s, during what has been referred to as the cola wars, soft-drink manufacturer Pepsi ran a series of advertisements where people, caught on hidden camera, in a blind taste test, chose Pepsi over rival Coca-Cola.

a. Cost per conversion
b. GL-70
c. Comparative advertising
d. Heavy-up

5. _____s is the social science that studies the production, distribution, and consumption of goods and services. The term _____s comes from the Ancient Greek oá¼°κονομῖα from oá¼¶κος (oikos, 'house') + vÏŒμος (nomos, 'custom' or 'law'), hence 'rules of the house(hold)'. Current _____ models developed out of the broader field of political economy in the late 19th century, owing to a desire to use an empirical approach more akin to the physical sciences.
   a. Economic
   b. Industrial organization
   c. ADTECH
   d. ACNielsen

6. _____ is one of the four Ps of the marketing mix. The other three aspects are product, promotion, and place. It is also a key variable in microeconomic price allocation theory.
   a. Competitor indexing
   b. Relationship based pricing
   c. Price
   d. Pricing

7. The _____ is an international organization whose stated aims are to facilitate cooperation in international law, international security, economic development, social progress, human rights and achieving world peace. The _____ was founded in 1945 after World War II to replace the League of Nations, to stop wars between countries and to provide a platform for dialogue.

There are currently 192 member states, including nearly every recognized independent state in the world.

   a. ADTECH
   b. ACNielsen
   c. AMAX
   d. United Nations

8. _____ is a mathematical science pertaining to the collection, analysis, interpretation or explanation, and presentation of data. It also provides tools for prediction and forecasting based on data. It is applicable to a wide variety of academic disciplines, from the natural and social sciences to the humanities, government and business.

a. Type I error
b. Null hypothesis
c. Statistics
d. Median

9. _____ in its literal sense is the process of transformation of local or regional phenomena into global ones. It can be described as a process by which the people of the world are unified into a single society and function together.

This process is a combination of economic, technological, sociocultural and political forces.

a. 180SearchAssistant
b. Power III
c. 6-3-5 Brainwriting
d. Globalization

10. _____ is defined by the American _____ Association as the activity, set of institutions, and processes for creating, communicating, delivering, and exchanging offerings that have value for customers, clients, partners, and society at large. The term developed from the original meaning which referred literally to going to market, as in shopping, or going to a market to sell goods or services.

_____ practice tends to be seen as a creative industry, which includes advertising, distribution and selling.

a. Customer acquisition management
b. Marketing
c. Product naming
d. Marketing myopia

11. _____ is a form of communication that typically attempts to persuade potential customers to purchase or to consume more of a particular brand of product or service. 'While now central to the contemporary global economy and the reproduction of global production networks, it is only quite recently that _____ has been more than a marginal influence on patterns of sales and production. The formation of modern _____ was intimately bound up with the emergence of new forms of monopoly capitalism around the end of the 19th and beginning of the 20th century as one element in corporate strategies to create, organize and where possible control markets, especially for mass produced consumer goods.

a. ADTECH
b. AMAX
c. ACNielsen
d. Advertising

12. Consumer market research is a form of applied sociology that concentrates on understanding the behaviours, whims and preferences, of consumers in a market-based economy, and aims to understand the effects and comparative success of marketing campaigns. The field of consumer _____ as a statistical science was pioneered by Arthur Nielsen with the founding of the ACNielsen Company in 1923.

Thus _____ is the systematic and objective identification, collection, analysis, and dissemination of information for the purpose of assisting management in decision making related to the identification and solution of problems and opportunities in marketing.

a. Focus group
b. Logit analysis
c. Marketing research process
d. Marketing research

13. _____ is difficult to define. For example, in 1952, Alfred Kroeber and Clyde Kluckhohn compiled a list of 164 definitions of '_____' in _____: A Critical Review of Concepts and Definitions. However, the word '_____' is most commonly used in three basic senses:

- excellence of taste in the fine arts and humanities
- an integrated pattern of human knowledge, belief, and behavior that depends upon the capacity for symbolic thought and social learning
- the set of shared attitudes, values, goals, and practices that characterizes an institution, organization or group.

When the concept first emerged in eighteenth- and nineteenth-century Europe, it connoted a process of cultivation or improvement, as in agriculture or horticulture. In the nineteenth century, it came to refer first to the betterment or refinement of the individual, especially through education, and then to the fulfillment of national aspirations or ideals.

a. Albert Einstein
b. Culture
c. AStore
d. African Americans

Chapter 2. The Essence of Marketing: Terms and Processes Nonprofits Need to Know

1. _____ is a term used to describe a person who was born during the demographic Post-World War II baby boom. Many analysts now believe that two distinct cultural generations were born during this baby boom; the older generation is often called the Baby Boom Generation and the younger generation is often called Generation Jones. The term '_____' is sometimes used in a cultural context, and sometimes used to describe someone who was born during the post-WWII baby boom.
   a. Greatest Generation
   b. Generation X
   c. AStore
   d. Baby Boomer

2. _____ was a writer, management consultant, and self-described 'social ecologist.' Widely considered to be the father of 'modern management,' his 39 books and countless scholarly and popular articles explored how humans are organized across all sectors of society--in business, government and the nonprofit world. His writings have predicted many of the major developments of the late twentieth century, including privatization and decentralization; the rise of Japan to economic world power; the decisive importance of marketing; and the emergence of the information society with its necessity of lifelong learning. In 1959, Drucker coined the term 'knowledge worker' and later in his life considered knowledge work productivity to be the next frontier of management.
   a. Paschal Eze
   b. Nouveau riche
   c. Rick Boyce
   d. Peter Ferdinand Drucker

3. _____ is defined by the American _____ Association as the activity, set of institutions, and processes for creating, communicating, delivering, and exchanging offerings that have value for customers, clients, partners, and society at large. The term developed from the original meaning which referred literally to going to market, as in shopping, or going to a market to sell goods or services.

   _____ practice tends to be seen as a creative industry, which includes advertising, distribution and selling.

   a. Customer acquisition management
   b. Marketing
   c. Product naming
   d. Marketing myopia

4. A _____ is a list of the general tasks and responsibilities of a position. Typically, it also includes to whom the position reports, specifications such as the qualifications needed by the person in the job, salary range for the position, etc. A _____ is usually developed by conducting a job analysis, which includes examining the tasks and sequences of tasks necessary to perform the job.

Chapter 2. The Essence of Marketing: Terms and Processes Nonprofits Need to Know

   a. 6-3-5 Brainwriting
   b. 180SearchAssistant
   c. Power III
   d. Job description

5. Competitiveness is a comparative concept of the ability and performance of a firm, sub-sector or country to sell and supply goods and/or services in a given market. Although widely used in economics and business management, the usefulness of the concept, particularly in the context of national competitiveness, is vigorously disputed by economists, such as Paul Krugman.

The term may also be applied to markets, where it is used to refer to the extent to which the market structure may be regarded as perfectly _____.

   a. Customs union
   b. Free trade zone
   c. Geographical pricing
   d. Competitive

6. _____ is, in very basic words, a position a firm occupies against its competitors.

According to Michael Porter, the three methods for creating a sustainable _____ are through:

1. Cost leadership - Cost advantage occurs when a firm delivers the same services as its competitors but at a lower cost;

2.

   a. Power III
   b. 6-3-5 Brainwriting
   c. 180SearchAssistant
   d. Competitive advantage

7. The _____ is a professional association for marketers. As of 2008 it had approximately 40,000 members. There are collegiate chapters on 250 campuses.
   a. AMAX
   b. American Marketing Association
   c. ADTECH
   d. ACNielsen

Chapter 2. The Essence of Marketing: Terms and Processes Nonprofits Need to Know

8. _____ is a broad label that refers to any individuals or households that use goods and services generated within the economy. The concept of a _____ is used in different contexts, so that the usage and significance of the term may vary.

A _____ is a person who uses any product or service.

   a. Power III
   b. Consumer
   c. 6-3-5 Brainwriting
   d. 180SearchAssistant

9. A _____ dominated business thought from the beginning of capitalism to the mid 1950s, and some argue it still exists in some industries. Business concerned itself primarily with production, manufacturing, and efficiency issues. Say's Law encapsulated this viewpoint, stating: 'Supply creates its own demand'.
   a. Blitz QFD
   b. Production orientation
   c. Product differentiation
   d. Marketing

10. _____ is an ongoing process that occurs strictly within a company or organization whereby the functional process aligns, motivates and empowers employees at all management levels to consistently deliver a satisfying customer experience. According to Burkitt and Zealley, 'the challenge for _____ is not only to get the right messages across, but to embed them in such a way that they both change and reinforce employee behaviour'.
   a. AMAX
   b. Internal marketing
   c. ACNielsen
   d. ADTECH

11. _____ is a rivalry between individuals, groups, nations for territory, a niche, or allocation of resources. It arises whenever two or more parties strive for a goal which cannot be shared. _____ occurs naturally between living organisms which co-exist in the same environment.
   a. Price fixing
   b. Price competition
   c. Competition
   d. Non-price competition

12. _____ is a term used in marketing as well as the title of an important marketing paper written by Theodore Levitt. This paper was first published in 1960 in the Harvard Business Review; a journal of which he was an editor.

Chapter 2. The Essence of Marketing: Terms and Processes Nonprofits Need to Know

Some commentators have suggested that its publication marked the beginning of the modern marketing movement.

a. Corporate image
b. Business marketing
c. Marketing performance measurement and management
d. Marketing myopia

13. _____ is a form of marketing developed from direct response marketing campaigns conducted in the 1970's and 1980's which emphasizes customer retention and satisfaction, rather than a dominant focus on 'point of sale' transactions.

_____ differs from other forms of marketing in that it recognizes the long term value to the firm of keeping customers, as opposed to direct or 'Intrusion' marketing, which focuses upon acquisition of new clients by targeting majority demographics based upon prospective client lists.

_____ refers to long-term and mutually beneficial arrangement wherein both buyer and seller focus on value enhancement through the certain of more satisfying exchange. This approach attempts to transcend the simple purchase exchange process with customer to make more meaningful and richer contact by providing a more holistic, personalized purchase, and use orn consumption experience to create stronger ties.

a. Guerrilla Marketing
b. Diversity marketing
c. Global marketing
d. Relationship marketing

14. In accounting, _____ has a very specific meaning. It is an outflow of cash or other valuable assets from a person or company to another person or company. This outflow of cash is generally one side of a trade for products or services that have equal or better current or future value to the buyer than to the seller.

a. ADTECH
b. ACNielsen
c. AMAX
d. Expense

15. _____ , according to The American Marketing Association, is 'a planning process designed to assure that all brand contacts received by a customer or prospect for a product, service, or organization are relevant to that person and consistent over time.' (Marketing Power Dictionary)

Chapter 2. The Essence of Marketing: Terms and Processes Nonprofits Need to Know

_____ is a term used to describe a holistic approach to marketing. It aims to ensure consistency of message and the complementary use of media. The concept includes online and offline marketing channels.

a. AMAX
b. ACNielsen
c. ADTECH
d. Integrated marketing communications

16. _____ or cause-related marketing refers to a type of marketing involving the cooperative efforts of a 'for profit' business and a non-profit organization for mutual benefit. The term is sometimes used more broadly and generally to refer to any type of marketing effort for social and other charitable causes, including in-house marketing efforts by non-profit organizations. _____ differs from corporate giving (philanthropy) as the latter generally involves a specific donation that is tax deductible, while _____ is a marketing relationship generally not based on a donation.

a. Global marketing
b. Cause-related Marketing
c. Cause marketing
d. Digital marketing

17. A _____ is a brief statement of the purpose of a company, organization. It is ideally used to guide the actions of the organization.

_____s often contain the following:

- Purpose of the organization
- The organization's primary stakeholders: clients, stockholders, etc.
- Responsibilities of the organization towards these stockholders
- Products and services offered

Generally shorter _____s are more effective than longer ones.

In developing a _____:

- Encourage input as feasible from employees, volunteers, and other stakeholders
- Publicize it broadly

The _____ can be used to resolve differences between business stakeholders. Stakeholders include: employees including managers and executives, stockholders, board of directors, customers, suppliers, distributors, creditors, governments (local, state, federal, etc.), unions, competitors, NGO's, and the general public.

Chapter 2. The Essence of Marketing: Terms and Processes Nonprofits Need to Know

  a. Power III
  b. 6-3-5 Brainwriting
  c. Mission statement
  d. 180SearchAssistant

18. Maslow's _____ is a theory in psychology, proposed by Abraham Maslow in his 1943 paper A Theory of Human Motivation, which he subsequently extended to include his observations of humans' innate curiosity.

Maslow studied what he called exemplary people such as Albert Einstein, Jane Addams, Eleanor Roosevelt, and Frederick Douglass rather than mentally ill or neurotic people, writing that 'the study of crippled, stunted, immature, and unhealthy specimens can yield only a cripple psychology and a cripple philosophy.' Maslow also studied the healthiest one percent of the college student population. In his book, The Farther Reaches of Human Nature, Maslow writes, 'By ordinary standards of this kind of laboratory research...

  a. 6-3-5 Brainwriting
  b. Power III
  c. 180SearchAssistant
  d. Hierarchy of needs

19. In economic models, the _____ time frame assumes no fixed factors of production. Firms can enter or leave the marketplace, and the cost (and availability) of land, labor, raw materials, and capital goods can be assumed to vary. In contrast, in the short-run time frame, certain factors are assumed to be fixed, because there is not sufficient time for them to change.
  a. 180SearchAssistant
  b. 6-3-5 Brainwriting
  c. Power III
  d. Long-run

20. A _____ is a process that can allow an organization to concentrate its limited resources on the greatest opportunities to increase sales and achieve a sustainable competitive advantage. A _____ should be centered around the key concept that customer satisfaction is the main goal.

A _____ is most effective when it is an integral component of corporate strategy, defining how the organization will successfully engage customers, prospects, and competitors in the market arena.

Chapter 2. The Essence of Marketing: Terms and Processes Nonprofits Need to Know

a. Cyberdoc
b. Psychographic
c. Societal marketing
d. Marketing strategy

21. A _____ is a plan of action designed to achieve a particular goal.

_____ is different from tactics. In military terms, tactics is concerned with the conduct of an engagement while _____ is concerned with how different engagements are linked.

a. Power III
b. 180SearchAssistant
c. 6-3-5 Brainwriting
d. Strategy

22. The phrase _____ refers to the aspect of corporate strategy, corporate finance and management dealing with the buying, selling and combining of different companies that can aid, finance, or help a growing company in a given industry grow rapidly without having to create another business entity.

An acquisition, also known as a takeover or a buyout, is the buying of one company (the 'target') by another. An acquisition may be friendly or hostile.

a. 6-3-5 Brainwriting
b. Power III
c. 180SearchAssistant
d. Mergers and acquisitions

23. Consumer market research is a form of applied sociology that concentrates on understanding the behaviours, whims and preferences, of consumers in a market-based economy, and aims to understand the effects and comparative success of marketing campaigns. The field of consumer _____ as a statistical science was pioneered by Arthur Nielsen with the founding of the ACNielsen Company in 1923.

Thus _____ is the systematic and objective identification, collection, analysis, and dissemination of information for the purpose of assisting management in decision making related to the identification and solution of problems and opportunities in marketing.

Chapter 2. The Essence of Marketing: Terms and Processes Nonprofits Need to Know

a. Marketing research process
b. Focus group
c. Logit analysis
d. Marketing research

24. _____ in organizations and public policy is both the organizational process of creating and maintaining a plan; and the psychological process of thinking about the activities required to create a desired goal on some scale. As such, it is a fundamental property of intelligent behavior. This thought process is essential to the creation and refinement of a plan, or integration of it with other plans, that is, it combines forecasting of developments with the preparation of scenarios of how to react to them.
   a. 6-3-5 Brainwriting
   b. Power III
   c. Planning
   d. 180SearchAssistant

25. In economics, an externality or spillover of an economic transaction is an impact on a party that is not directly involved in the transaction. In such a case, prices do not reflect the full costs or benefits in production or consumption of a product or service. A positive impact is called an _____ benefit, while a negative impact is called an _____ cost.
   a. ADTECH
   b. ACNielsen
   c. External
   d. AMAX

26. _____ is a strategic planning method used to evaluate the Strengths, Weaknesses, Opportunities, and Threats involved in a project or in a business venture. It involves specifying the objective of the business venture or project and identifying the internal and external factors that are favorable and unfavorable to achieving that objective. The technique is credited to Albert Humphrey, who led a research project at Stanford University in the 1960s and 1970s using data from Fortune 500 companies.
   a. Product differentiation
   b. Lead scoring
   c. SWOT analysis
   d. Market environment

Chapter 2. The Essence of Marketing: Terms and Processes Nonprofits Need to Know

27. _____ is a marketing term, and involves evaluating the situation and trends in a particular company's market. _____ is often called the 'three c's', which refers to the three major elements that must be studied:

- Customers
- Costs
- Competition

The number of 'c's' is sometimes extended to four, five, or even six, with 'Collaboration', 'Company', and 'Competitive advantage'.

- Marketing mix
- SWOT analysis

a. 180SearchAssistant
b. Situation analysis
c. 6-3-5 Brainwriting
d. Power III

28. _____ is a business term meaning the market segment to which a particular good or service is marketed. It is mainly defined by age, gender, geography, socio-economic grouping, technographic, or any other combination of demographics. It is generally studied and mapped by an organization through lists and reports containing demographic information that may have an effect on the marketing of key products or services.

a. Category Development Index
b. Distribution
c. Brando
d. Market specialization

29. The _____ is generally accepted as the use and specification of the four p's describing the strategic position of a product in the marketplace. One version of the origins of the _____ starts in 1948 when James Culliton said that a marketing decision should be a result of something similar to a recipe. This version continued in 1953 when Neil Borden, in his American Marketing Association presidential address, took the recipe idea one step further and coined the term 'Marketing-Mix'.

a. Power III
b. Marketing mix
c. 180SearchAssistant
d. 6-3-5 Brainwriting

Chapter 2. The Essence of Marketing: Terms and Processes Nonprofits Need to Know

30. A _____ or logistics network is the system of organizations, people, technology, activities, information and resources involved in moving a product or service from supplier to customer. _____ activities transform natural resources, raw materials and components into a finished product that is delivered to the end customer. In sophisticated _____ systems, used products may re-enter the _____ at any point where residual value is recyclable.
    a. Demand chain management
    b. Purchasing
    c. Supply chain network
    d. Supply chain

31. _____ is a form of communication that typically attempts to persuade potential customers to purchase or to consume more of a particular brand of product or service. 'While now central to the contemporary global economy and the reproduction of global production networks, it is only quite recently that _____ has been more than a marginal influence on patterns of sales and production. The formation of modern _____ was intimately bound up with the emergence of new forms of monopoly capitalism around the end of the 19th and beginning of the 20th century as one element in corporate strategies to create, organize and where possible control markets, especially for mass produced consumer goods.
    a. ADTECH
    b. Advertising
    c. AMAX
    d. ACNielsen

32. _____ is the realization of an application idea, model, design, specification, standard, algorithm an _____ is a realization of a technical specification or algorithm as a program, software component, or other computer system. Many _____s may exist for a given specification or standard.
    a. ADTECH
    b. Implementation
    c. ACNielsen
    d. AMAX

33. _____ is one of the four Ps of the marketing mix. The other three aspects are product, promotion, and place. It is also a key variable in microeconomic price allocation theory.
    a. Relationship based pricing
    b. Competitor indexing
    c. Price
    d. Pricing

Chapter 2. The Essence of Marketing: Terms and Processes Nonprofits Need to Know

34. _____ involves disseminating information about a product, product line, brand, or company. It is one of the four key aspects of the marketing mix. (The other three elements are product marketing, pricing, and distribution). P>_____ is generally sub-divided into two parts:

- Above the line _____: Promotion in the media (e.g. TV, radio, newspapers, Internet and Mobile Phones) in which the advertiser pays an advertising agency to place the ad
- Below the line _____: All other _____. Much of this is intended to be subtle enough for the consumer to be unaware that _____ is taking place. E.g. sponsorship, product placement, endorsements, sales _____, merchandising, direct mail, personal selling, public relations, trade shows

a. Davie Brown Index
b. Cashmere Agency
c. Bottling lines
d. Promotion

35. _____ generally refers to a list of all planned expenses and revenues. It is a plan for saving and spending. A _____ is an important concept in microeconomics, which uses a _____ line to illustrate the trade-offs between two or more goods.
a. 6-3-5 Brainwriting
b. 180SearchAssistant
c. Power III
d. Budget

36. _____ is difficult to define. For example, in 1952, Alfred Kroeber and Clyde Kluckhohn compiled a list of 164 definitions of '_____' in _____: A Critical Review of Concepts and Definitions. However, the word '_____' is most commonly used in three basic senses:

- excellence of taste in the fine arts and humanities
- an integrated pattern of human knowledge, belief, and behavior that depends upon the capacity for symbolic thought and social learning
- the set of shared attitudes, values, goals, and practices that characterizes an institution, organization or group.

When the concept first emerged in eighteenth- and nineteenth-century Europe, it connoted a process of cultivation or improvement, as in agriculture or horticulture. In the nineteenth century, it came to refer first to the betterment or refinement of the individual, especially through education, and then to the fulfillment of national aspirations or ideals.

a. Albert Einstein
b. AStore
c. African Americans
d. Culture

Chapter 3. Approaching the Market

1. Maslow's _____ is a theory in psychology, proposed by Abraham Maslow in his 1943 paper A Theory of Human Motivation, which he subsequently extended to include his observations of humans' innate curiosity.

Maslow studied what he called exemplary people such as Albert Einstein, Jane Addams, Eleanor Roosevelt, and Frederick Douglass rather than mentally ill or neurotic people, writing that 'the study of crippled, stunted, immature, and unhealthy specimens can yield only a cripple psychology and a cripple philosophy.' Maslow also studied the healthiest one percent of the college student population. In his book, The Farther Reaches of Human Nature, Maslow writes, 'By ordinary standards of this kind of laboratory research...

   a. 180SearchAssistant
   b. Power III
   c. 6-3-5 Brainwriting
   d. Hierarchy of needs

2. _____ is a broad label that refers to any individuals or households that use goods and services generated within the economy. The concept of a _____ is used in different contexts, so that the usage and significance of the term may vary.

A _____ is a person who uses any product or service.

   a. Consumer
   b. Power III
   c. 6-3-5 Brainwriting
   d. 180SearchAssistant

3. _____ is the study of when, why, how, where and what people do or do not buy products. It blends elements from psychology, sociology, social psychology, anthropology and economics. It attempts to understand the buyer decision making process, both individually and in groups. It studies characteristics of individual consumers such as demographics and behavioural variables in an attempt to understand people's wants. It also tries to assess influences on the consumer from groups such as family, friends, reference groups, and society in general.
   a. Communal marketing
   b. Consumer behavior
   c. Consumer confidence
   d. Multidimensional scaling

4. In economics, a _____ exists when a specific individual or enterprise has sufficient control over a particular product or service to determine significantly the terms on which other individuals shall have access to it. Monopolies are thus characterized by a lack of economic competition for the good or service that they provide and a lack of viable substitute goods. The verb 'monopolize' refers to the process by which a firm gains persistently greater market share than what is expected under perfect competition.

Chapter 3. Approaching the Market

   a. 6-3-5 Brainwriting
   b. 180SearchAssistant
   c. Power III
   d. Monopoly

5. An _____ is a market form in which a market or industry is dominated by a small number of sellers (oligopolists.) Because there are few participants in this type of market, each oligopolist is aware of the actions of the others. The decisions of one firm influence, and are influenced by, the decisions of other firms.
   a. ACNielsen
   b. Oligopoly
   c. ADTECH
   d. AMAX

6. _____ is a rivalry between individuals, groups, nations for territory, a niche, or allocation of resources. It arises whenever two or more parties strive for a goal which cannot be shared. _____ occurs naturally between living organisms which co-exist in the same environment.
   a. Competition
   b. Price fixing
   c. Price competition
   d. Non-price competition

7. _____s is the social science that studies the production, distribution, and consumption of goods and services. The term _____s comes from the Ancient Greek οἰκονομία from οἶκος (oikos, 'house') + νόμος (nomos, 'custom' or 'law'), hence 'rules of the house(hold)'. Current _____ models developed out of the broader field of political economy in the late 19th century, owing to a desire to use an empirical approach more akin to the physical sciences.
   a. ACNielsen
   b. ADTECH
   c. Economic
   d. Industrial organization

8. A _____ is a company or individual that purchases goods or services with the intention of reselling them rather than consuming or using them. This is usually done for profit (but could be resold at a loss.) One example can be found in the industry of telecommunications, where companies buy excess amounts of transmission capacity or call time from other carriers and resell it to smaller carriers.

Chapter 3. Approaching the Market

a. Discontinuation
b. Value-based pricing
c. Jobbing house
d. Reseller

9. _____ is a business term meaning the market segment to which a particular good or service is marketed. It is mainly defined by age, gender, geography, socio-economic grouping, technographic, or any other combination of demographics. It is generally studied and mapped by an organization through lists and reports containing demographic information that may have an effect on the marketing of key products or services.

   a. Distribution
   b. Market specialization
   c. Brando
   d. Category Development Index

10. _____? is an American advertising campaign encouraging the consumption of cow's milk, which was created by the advertising agency Goodby Silverstein ' Partners for the California Milk Processor Board in 1993 and later licensed for use by milk processors and dairy farmers. It has been running since October 1993. The campaign has been credited with greatly increasing milk sales nationwide after a 20-year slump.

    a. Got Milk?
    b. Who Makes Movies?
    c. You Got the Right One, Baby
    d. Slip-Slop-Slap

11. In marketing, _____ is the process of distinguishing the differences of a product or offering from others, to make it more attractive to a particular target market. This involves differentiating it from competitors' products as well as one's own product offerings.

Differentiation is a source of competitive advantage.

   a. Product differentiation
   b. Packshot
   c. Marketing myopia
   d. Corporate image

12. A _____ is a plan of action designed to achieve a particular goal.

_____ is different from tactics. In military terms, tactics is concerned with the conduct of an engagement while _____ is concerned with how different engagements are linked.

Chapter 3. Approaching the Market

a. 6-3-5 Brainwriting
b. Power III
c. Strategy
d. 180SearchAssistant

13. _____ is the study of the Earth and its lands, features, inhabitants, and phenomena. A literal translation would be 'to describe or write about the Earth'. The first person to use the word '_____' was Eratosthenes .
   a. Geography
   b. 6-3-5 Brainwriting
   c. Power III
   d. 180SearchAssistant

14. _____ or _____ data refers to selected population characteristics as used in government, marketing or opinion research, or the _____ profiles used in such research. Note the distinction from the term 'demography' Commonly-used _____ include race, age, income, disabilities, mobility (in terms of travel time to work or number of vehicles available), educational attainment, home ownership, employment status, and even location.
   a. Albert Einstein
   b. AStore
   c. African Americans
   d. Demographic

15. In economics, an externality or spillover of an economic transaction is an impact on a party that is not directly involved in the transaction. In such a case, prices do not reflect the full costs or benefits in production or consumption of a product or service. A positive impact is called an _____ benefit, while a negative impact is called an _____ cost.
   a. AMAX
   b. ACNielsen
   c. External
   d. ADTECH

16. A _____ is a subgroup of people or organizations sharing one or more characteristics that cause them to have similar product and/or service needs. A true _____ meets all of the following criteria: it is distinct from other segments (different segments have different needs), it is homogeneous within the segment (exhibits common needs); it responds similarly to a market stimulus, and it can be reached by a market intervention. The term is also used when consumers with identical product and/or service needs are divided up into groups so they can be charged different amounts.

a. Customer insight
b. Commercial planning
c. Market segment
d. Production orientation

17. _____ was originally coined by Austrian psychologist Alfred Adler in 1929. The current broader sense of the word dates from 1961.

In sociology, a _____ is the way a person lives.

a. 6-3-5 Brainwriting
b. Power III
c. 180SearchAssistant
d. Lifestyle

18. The phrase _____, according to the Organization for Economic Co-operation and Development, refers to 'creative work undertaken on a systematic basis in order to increase the stock of knowledge, including knowledge of man, culture and society, and the use of this stock of knowledge to devise new applications [sic]' Though it is questionable that an organization is needed for this definition, as it is quite obvious that _____ refers to the _____ of something.

New product design and development is more often than not a crucial factor in the survival of a company. In an industry that is fast changing, firms must continually revise their design and range of products.

a. 6-3-5 Brainwriting
b. 180SearchAssistant
c. Power III
d. Research and development

19. _____ is systematic determination of merit, worth, and significance of something or someone using criteria against a set of standards. _____ often is used to characterize and appraise subjects of interest in a wide range of human enterprises, including the arts, criminal justice, foundations and non-profit organizations, government, health care, and other human services.

Depending on the topic of interest, there are professional groups which look to the quality and rigor of the _____ process.

Chapter 3. Approaching the Market

a. ACNielsen
b. ADTECH
c. AMAX
d. Evaluation

20. In economics, _____ is the desire to own something and the ability to pay for it. The term _____ signifies the ability or the willingness to buy a particular commodity at a given point of time.

a. Market dominance
b. Discretionary spending
c. Market system
d. Demand

21. _____ is one of the four Ps of the marketing mix. The other three aspects are product, promotion, and place. It is also a key variable in microeconomic price allocation theory.

a. Relationship based pricing
b. Price
c. Competitor indexing
d. Pricing

22. In marketing, _____ has come to mean the process by which marketers try to create an image or identity in the minds of their target market for its product, brand, or organization. It is the 'relative competitive comparison' their product occupies in a given market as perceived by the target market.

Re-_____ involves changing the identity of a product, relative to the identity of competing products, in the collective minds of the target market.

a. Positioning
b. Containerization
c. Moratorium
d. GE matrix

23. Competitiveness is a comparative concept of the ability and performance of a firm, sub-sector or country to sell and supply goods and/or services in a given market. Although widely used in economics and business management, the usefulness of the concept, particularly in the context of national competitiveness, is vigorously disputed by economists, such as Paul Krugman.

The term may also be applied to markets, where it is used to refer to the extent to which the market structure may be regarded as perfectly _____.

   a. Customs union
   b. Free trade zone
   c. Geographical pricing
   d. Competitive

Chapter 4. Marketing Research: The Foundation for Planning

1. _____ is defined by the American _____ Association as the activity, set of institutions, and processes for creating, communicating, delivering, and exchanging offerings that have value for customers, clients, partners, and society at large. The term developed from the original meaning which referred literally to going to market, as in shopping, or going to a market to sell goods or services.

   _____ practice tends to be seen as a creative industry, which includes advertising, distribution and selling.

   a. Marketing myopia
   b. Customer acquisition management
   c. Product naming
   d. Marketing

2. Consumer market research is a form of applied sociology that concentrates on understanding the behaviours, whims and preferences, of consumers in a market-based economy, and aims to understand the effects and comparative success of marketing campaigns. The field of consumer _____ as a statistical science was pioneered by Arthur Nielsen with the founding of the ACNielsen Company in 1923.

   Thus _____ is the systematic and objective identification, collection, analysis, and dissemination of information for the purpose of assisting management in decision making related to the identification and solution of problems and opportunities in marketing.

   a. Marketing research
   b. Focus group
   c. Marketing research process
   d. Logit analysis

3. _____ often refers to either primary or secondary research. Secondary research involves a company using information compiled from various sources, which is about a new or existing product. The advantages of secondary research are that it is relatively cheap and easily accessible.
   a. Questionnaire
   b. Mystery shoppers
   c. Mystery shopping
   d. Market research

4. _____ is a broad label that refers to any individuals or households that use goods and services generated within the economy. The concept of a _____ is used in different contexts, so that the usage and significance of the term may vary.

   A _____ is a person who uses any product or service.

Chapter 4. Marketing Research: The Foundation for Planning

  a. 6-3-5 Brainwriting
  b. Consumer
  c. Power III
  d. 180SearchAssistant

5. _____ is a form of communication that typically attempts to persuade potential customers to purchase or to consume more of a particular brand of product or service. 'While now central to the contemporary global economy and the reproduction of global production networks, it is only quite recently that _____ has been more than a marginal influence on patterns of sales and production. The formation of modern _____ was intimately bound up with the emergence of new forms of monopoly capitalism around the end of the 19th and beginning of the 20th century as one element in corporate strategies to create, organize and where possible control markets, especially for mass produced consumer goods.
  a. AMAX
  b. Advertising
  c. ADTECH
  d. ACNielsen

6. _____ deals with the first of the '4P''s of marketing, which are Product, Pricing, Place, and Promotion. _____, as opposed to product management, deals with more outbound marketing tasks. For example, product management deals with the nuts and bolts of product development within a firm, whereas _____ deals with marketing the product to prospects, customers, and others.
  a. Crisis management
  b. Reverse hierarchy
  c. Corporate transparency
  d. Product marketing

7. _____ involves disseminating information about a product, product line, brand, or company. It is one of the four key aspects of the marketing mix. (The other three elements are product marketing, pricing, and distribution). P>_____ is generally sub-divided into two parts:

  - Above the line _____: Promotion in the media (e.g. TV, radio, newspapers, Internet and Mobile Phones) in which the advertiser pays an advertising agency to place the ad
  - Below the line _____: All other _____. Much of this is intended to be subtle enough for the consumer to be unaware that _____ is taking place. E.g. sponsorship, product placement, endorsements, sales _____, merchandising, direct mail, personal selling, public relations, trade shows

a. Bottling lines
b. Cashmere Agency
c. Promotion
d. Davie Brown Index

8. A number of different _____s are indicated below.

   - Randomized controlled trial
     - Double-blind randomized trial
     - Single-blind randomized trial
     - Non-blind trial
   - Nonrandomized trial (quasi-experiment)
     - Interrupted time series design (measures on a sample or a series of samples from the same population are obtained several times before and after a manipulated event or a naturally occurring event) - considered a type of quasi-experiment
   - Cohort study
     - Prospective cohort
     - Retrospective cohort
     - Time series study
   - Case-control study
     - Nested case-control study
   - Cross-sectional study
     - Community survey (a type of cross-sectional study)

When choosing a _____, many factors must be taken into account. Different types of studies are subject to different types of bias. For example, recall bias is likely to occur in cross-sectional or case-control studies where subjects are asked to recall exposure to risk factors.

a. Study design
b. Power III
c. Longitudinal studies
d. 180SearchAssistant

9. _____ refer to a collection of facts usually collected as the result of experience, observation or experiment or a set of premises. This may consist of numbers, words particularly as measurements or observations of a set of variables. _____ are often viewed as a lowest level of abstraction from which information and knowledge are derived.

a. Mean
b. Sample size
c. Pearson product-moment correlation coefficient
d. Data

10. A _____ in programming languages is an attribute of a data which tells the computer (and the programmer) something about the kind of data it is. This involves setting constraints on the datum, such as what values it can take and what operations may be performed upon it.

In a broad sense, a _____ defines a set of values and the allowable operations on those values.

a. 6-3-5 Brainwriting
b. Power III
c. Data type
d. 180SearchAssistant

11. A _____ is a structured collection of records or data that is stored in a computer system. The structure is achieved by organizing the data according to a _____ model. The model in most common use today is the relational model.

a. 180SearchAssistant
b. 6-3-5 Brainwriting
c. Power III
d. Database

12. _____ is a term used to describe a process of preparing and collecting data - for example as part of a process improvement or similar project.

_____ usually takes place early on in an improvement project, and is often formalised through a _____ Plan which often contains the following activity.

1. Pre collection activity - Agree goals, target data, definitions, methods
2. Collection - _____
3. Present Findings - usually involves some form of sorting analysis and/or presentation.

Chapter 4. Marketing Research: The Foundation for Planning

A formal _____ process is necessary as it ensures that data gathered is both defined and accurate and that subsequent decisions based on arguments embodied in the findings are valid . The process provides both a baseline from which to measure from and in certain cases a target on what to improve. Types of _____ 1-By mail questionnaires 2-By personal interview

- Six sigma
- Sampling (statistics)

a. 6-3-5 Brainwriting
b. Power III
c. 180SearchAssistant
d. Data collection

13. In statistics, an _____ draws inferences about the effect of a treatment on subjects, where the assignment of subjects into a treated group versus a control group is outside the control of the investigator. This is in contrast with controlled experiments, such as randomized controlled trials, where each subject is randomly assigned to a treated group or a control group before the start of the treatment.

The assignment of treatments may be beyond the control of the investigator for a variety of reasons:

- A randomized experiment would violate ethical standards. Suppose one wanted to investigate the abortion-breast cancer hypothesis, which postulates a causal link between induced abortion and the incidence of breast cancer. In a hypothetical controlled experiment, one would start with a large subject pool of pregnant women and divide them randomly into a treatment group (receiving induced abortions) and a control group (bearing children), and then conduct regular cancer screenings for women from both groups. Needless to say, such an experiment would run counter to common ethical principles. (It would also suffer from various confounds and sources of bias, e.g., it would be impossible to conduct it as a blind experiment.) The published studies investigating the abortion-breast cancer hypothesis generally start with a group of women who already have received abortions. Membership in this 'treated' group is not controlled by the investigator: the group is formed after the 'treatment' has been assigned.

- The investigator may simply lack the requisite influence. Suppose a scientist wants to study the public health effects of a community-wide ban on smoking in public indoor areas.

a. Observational study
b. AMAX
c. ACNielsen
d. ADTECH

Chapter 4. Marketing Research: The Foundation for Planning

14. A _____ is a research instrument consisting of a series of questions and other prompts for the purpose of gathering information from respondents. Although they are often designed for statistical analysis of the responses, this is not always the case. The _____ was invented by Sir Francis Galton.
    a. Market research
    b. Mystery shoppers
    c. Mystery shopping
    d. Questionnaire

15. A _____ is a form of qualitative research in which a group of people are asked about their attitude towards a product, service, concept, advertisement, idea, or packaging. Questions are asked in an interactive group setting where participants are free to talk with other group members.

    Ernest Dichter originated the idea of having a 'group therapy' for products and this process is what became known as a _____.

    a. Focus group
    b. Marketing research process
    c. Logit analysis
    d. Cross tabulation

16. _____ are a class of semi-structured projective techniques. _____ typically provide respondents with beginnings of sentences, referred to as 'stems,' and respondents then complete the sentences in ways that are meaningful to them. The responses are believed to provide indications of attitudes, beliefs, motivations, or other mental states.
    a. Response rate
    b. Reference value
    c. Power III
    d. Sentence completion tests

17. _____ is a common word game involving an exchange of words that are associated together.

    Once an original word has been chosen, usually randomly or arbitrarily, a player will find a word that they associate with it and make it known to all the players, usually by saying it aloud or writing it down as the next item on a list of words so far used. The next player must then do the same with this previous word.

    a. 180SearchAssistant
    b. 6-3-5 Brainwriting
    c. Power III
    d. Word association

18. _____ is a way of expressing knowledge or belief that an event will occur or has occurred. In mathematics the concept has been given an exact meaning in _____ theory, that is used extensively in such areas of study as mathematics, statistics, finance, gambling, science, and philosophy to draw conclusions about the likelihood of potential events and the underlying mechanics of complex systems.
   a. Probability
   b. Heteroskedastic
   c. Data
   d. Linear regression

19. A sample is a subject chosen from a population for investigation. A _____ is one chosen by a method involving an unpredictable component. Random sampling can also refer to taking a number of independent observations from the same probability distribution, without involving any real population.
   a. Power III
   b. Selection bias
   c. 180SearchAssistant
   d. Random sample

20. A personal and cultural _____ is a relative ethic _____, an assumption upon which implementation can be extrapolated. A _____ system is a set of consistent _____s and measures that is soo not true. A principle _____ is a foundation upon which other _____s and measures of integrity are based.
   a. Supreme Court of the United States
   b. Perceptual maps
   c. Package-on-Package
   d. Value

21. In economics, business, retail, and accounting, a _____ is the value of money that has been used up to produce something, and hence is not available for use anymore. In economics, a _____ is an alternative that is given up as a result of a decision. In business, the _____ may be one of acquisition, in which case the amount of money expended to acquire it is counted as _____.
   a. Fixed costs
   b. Variable cost
   c. Transaction cost
   d. Cost

Chapter 5. External Considerations in Marketing Introduction

1. In economics, an externality or spillover of an economic transaction is an impact on a party that is not directly involved in the transaction. In such a case, prices do not reflect the full costs or benefits in production or consumption of a product or service. A positive impact is called an _____ benefit, while a negative impact is called an _____ cost.
   a. ADTECH
   b. External
   c. AMAX
   d. ACNielsen

2. _____ is a process of gathering, analyzing, and dispensing information for tactical or strategic purposes. The _____ process entails obtaining both factual and subjective information on the business environments in which a company is operating or considering entering.

There are three ways of scanning the business environment:

- Ad-hoc scanning - Short term, infrequent examinations usually initiated by a crisis
- Regular scanning - Studies done on a regular schedule (say, once a year)
- Continuous scanning(also called continuous learning) - continuous structured data collection and processing on a broad range of environmental factors

Most commentators feel that in today's turbulent business environment the best scanning method available is continuous scanning.This allows the firm to :

-act quickly-take advantage of opportunities before competitors do-respond to environmental threats before significant damage is done

The Macro Environment

_____ usually refers just to the macro environment, but it can also include:-industry -competitor analysis -marketing research(consumer analysis) -New Product Development(product innovations)- the company's internal environment

Macro _____ involves analysing:

- The Economy

GDP per capitaeconomic growthunemployment]] rateinflation]] rateconsumer and investor confidenceinventory levelscurrency exchange ratesmerchandise trade balancefinancial and political health of trading partnersbalance of paymentsfuture trends

- Government

Chapter 5. External Considerations in Marketing Introduction

political climate - amount of government activitypolitical stability and riskgovernment debtbudget deficit or surpluscorporate and personal tax ratespayroll taxesimport tariffs and quotasexport restrictionsrestrictions on international financial flows

- Legal

minimum wage lawsenvironmental protection lawsworker safety lawsunion lawscopyright and patent lawsanti- monopoly lawsSunday closing lawsmunicipal licenceslaws that favour business investment

- Technology

Chapter 5. External Considerations in Marketing Introduction

efficiency of infrastructure, including: roads, ports, airports, rolling stock, hospitals, education, healthcare, communication, etc.industrial productivitynew manufacturing processesnew products and services of competitorsnew products and services of supply chain partnersany new technology that could impact the companycost and accessibility of electrical power

- Ecology
    - ecological concerns that affect the firms production processes
    - ecological concerns that affect customers' buying habits
    - ecological concerns that affect customers' perception of the company or product
- Socio-Cultural
    - demographic factors such as:
        - population size and distribution
        - age distribution
        - education levels
        - income levels
        - ethnic origins
        - religious affiliations
    - attitudes towards:
        - materialism, capitalism, free enterprise
        - individualism, role of family, role of government, collectivism
        - role of church and religion
        - consumerism
        - environmentalism
        - importance of work, pride of accomplishment
    - cultural structures including:
        - diet and nutrition
        - housing conditions
- Potential Suppliers
    - Labour supply
        - quantity of labour available
        - quality of labour available
        - stability of labour supply
        - wage expectations
        - employee turn-over rate
        - strikes and labour relations
        - educational facilities
    - Material suppliers
        - quality, quantity, price, and stability of material inputs
        - delivery delays
        - proximity of bulky or heavy material inputs
        - level of competition among suppliers
    - Service Providers
        - quantity, quality, price, and stability of service facilitators
        - special requirements
- Stakeholders
    - Lobbyists
    - Shareholders
    - Employees
    - Partners

Scanning these macro environmental variables for threats and opportunities requires that each issue be rated on two dimensions. It must be rated on its potential impact on the company, and rated on its likeliness of occurrence.

a. AMAX
b. ADTECH
c. ACNielsen
d. Environmental scanning

3. Competitiveness is a comparative concept of the ability and performance of a firm, sub-sector or country to sell and supply goods and/or services in a given market. Although widely used in economics and business management, the usefulness of the concept, particularly in the context of national competitiveness, is vigorously disputed by economists, such as Paul Krugman.

The term may also be applied to markets, where it is used to refer to the extent to which the market structure may be regarded as perfectly _____.

a. Competitive
b. Free trade zone
c. Customs union
d. Geographical pricing

4. _____ is a rivalry between individuals, groups, nations for territory, a niche, or allocation of resources. It arises whenever two or more parties strive for a goal which cannot be shared. _____ occurs naturally between living organisms which co-exist in the same environment.

a. Non-price competition
b. Price fixing
c. Price competition
d. Competition

5. _____ is a broad label that refers to any individuals or households that use goods and services generated within the economy. The concept of a _____ is used in different contexts, so that the usage and significance of the term may vary.

A _____ is a person who uses any product or service.

a. 6-3-5 Brainwriting
b. 180SearchAssistant
c. Power III
d. Consumer

6. In economics, _____ is the use of government spending and revenue collection to influence the economy.

_____ can be contrasted with the other main type of economic policy, monetary policy, which attempts to stabilize the economy by controlling interest rates and the supply of money. The two main instruments of _____ are government spending and taxation.

a. Monetary policy
b. Power III
c. Tariff
d. Fiscal policy

7. _____ is the process by which the government, central bank (ii) availability of money, and (iii) cost of money or rate of interest, in order to attain a set of objectives oriented towards the growth and stability of the economy. Monetary theory provides insight into how to craft optimal _____.

_____ is referred to as either being an expansionary policy where an expansionary policy increases the total supply of money in the economy, and a contractionary policy decreases the total money supply.

a. Tariff
b. Power III
c. Fiscal policy
d. Monetary policy

8. A supply chain is the system of organizations, people, technology, activities, information and resources involved in moving a product or service from _____ to customer. Supply chain activities transform natural resources, raw materials and components into a finished product that is delivered to the end customer. In sophisticated supply chain systems, used products may re-enter the supply chain at any point where residual value is recyclable.

a. Supplier
b. Product line extension
c. Rebate
d. Bringin' Home the Oil

Chapter 5. External Considerations in Marketing Introduction

9. _____ is the area of law in which manufacturers, distributors, suppliers, retailers, and others who make products available to the public are held responsible for the injuries those products cause.

In the United States, the claims most commonly associated with _____ are negligence, strict liability, breach of warranty, and various consumer protection claims. The majority of _____ laws are determined at the state level and vary widely from state to state.

 a. Product liability
 b. Registered trademark symbol
 c. Mediation
 d. Trespass to land

10. Regulation refers to 'controlling human or societal behaviour by rules or restrictions.' Regulation can take many forms: legal restrictions promulgated by a government authority, self-regulation, social regulation (e.g. norms), co-regulation and market regulation. One can consider regulation as actions of conduct imposing sanctions (such as a fine.) This action of administrative law, or implementing _____ law, may be contrasted with statutory or case law.
 a. Robinson-Patman Act
 b. Right to Financial Privacy Act
 c. Regulatory
 d. Privacy law

11. _____ is a form of government regulation which protects the interests of consumers. For example, a government may require businesses to disclose detailed information about products--particularly in areas where safety or public health is an issue, such as food. _____ is linked to the idea of consumer rights (that consumers have various rights as consumers), and to the formation of consumer organizations which help consumers make better choices in the marketplace.
 a. Sound trademark
 b. Trademark dilution
 c. Federal Bureau of Investigation
 d. Consumer protection

12. _____ is a process by which government's control over businesses and individuals is reduced or eliminated. It is the removal of some governmental controls over a market. _____ does not mean elimination of laws against fraud, but eliminating or reducing government control of how business is done, thereby moving toward a more free market.
 a. Consumer spending
 b. Value added
 c. Power III
 d. Deregulation

Chapter 5. External Considerations in Marketing Introduction

13. _____ refers to 'controlling human or societal behaviour by rules or restrictions.' _____ can take many forms: legal restrictions promulgated by a government authority, self-_____, social _____, co-_____ and market _____. One can consider _____ as actions of conduct imposing sanctions (such as a fine.) This action of administrative law, or implementing regulatory law, may be contrasted with statutory or case law.
    a. Rule of four
    b. Non-conventional trademark
    c. Regulation
    d. CAN-SPAM

14. _____ is the equation of personal happiness with consumption and the purchase of material possessions.

The term is often associated with criticisms of consumption starting with Thorstein Veblen.

Veblen's subject of examination, the newly emergent middle class arising at the turn of the twentieth century, comes to full fruition by the end of the twentieth century through the process of globalization.

In economics, _____ refers to economic policies placing emphasis on consumption.

   a. 180SearchAssistant
   b. Power III
   c. 6-3-5 Brainwriting
   d. Consumerism

15. _____ is a branch of philosophy which seeks to address questions about morality, such as how a moral outcome can be achieved in a specific situation (applied _____), how moral values should be determined (normative _____), what moral values people actually abide by (descriptive _____), what the fundamental semantic, ontological, and epistemic nature of _____ or morality is (meta-_____), and how moral capacity or moral agency develops and what its nature is (moral psychology.)

Socrates was one of the first Greek philosophers to encourage both scholars and the common citizen to turn their attention from the outside world to the condition of man. In this view, Knowledge having a bearing on human life was placed highest, all other knowledge being secondary.

   a. Ethics
   b. AMAX
   c. ACNielsen
   d. ADTECH

16. _____ is gross income minus income tax on that income.

Chapter 5. External Considerations in Marketing Introduction

Discretionary income is income after subtracting taxes and normal expenses (such as rent or mortgage and food) to maintain a certain standard of living. It is the amount of an individual's income available for spending after the essentials (such as food, clothing, and shelter) have been taken care of:

Discretionary income = Gross income - taxes - necessities

Despite the formal definitions above, _____ is commonly used to denote Discretionary income.

a. Disposable income
b. Power III
c. 6-3-5 Brainwriting
d. 180SearchAssistant

17. _____s is the social science that studies the production, distribution, and consumption of goods and services. The term _____s comes from the Ancient Greek oá¼°κονομῐα from oá¼¶κος (oikos, 'house') + vĺŒμος (nomos, 'custom' or 'law'), hence 'rules of the house(hold)'. Current _____ models developed out of the broader field of political economy in the late 19th century, owing to a desire to use an empirical approach more akin to the physical sciences.
   a. ACNielsen
   b. Industrial organization
   c. ADTECH
   d. Economic

18. The _____ concept is an enlightened marketing concept that holds that a company should make good marketing decisions by considering consumers' wants, the company's requirements, and society's long-term interests. It is closely linked with the principles of corporate social responsibility and of sustainable development.

The concept has an emphasis on social responsibility and suggests that for a company to only focus on exchange relationship with customers might not be suitable in order to sustain long term success.

   a. Marketing
   b. Customer franchise
   c. Societal marketing
   d. Business-to-business

19. _____ is defined by the American _____ Association as the activity, set of institutions, and processes for creating, communicating, delivering, and exchanging offerings that have value for customers, clients, partners, and society at large. The term developed from the original meaning which referred literally to going to market, as in shopping, or going to a market to sell goods or services.

Chapter 5. External Considerations in Marketing Introduction

_____ practice tends to be seen as a creative industry, which includes advertising, distribution and selling.

a. Product naming
b. Customer acquisition management
c. Marketing myopia
d. Marketing

20. The term _____ refers to economy-wide fluctuations in production or economic activity over several months or years. These fluctuations occur around a long-term growth trend, and typically involve shifts over time between periods of relatively rapid economic growth (expansion or boom), and periods of relative stagnation or decline (contraction or recession.)

These fluctuations are often measured using the growth rate of real gross domestic product.

a. Market structure
b. Monopolistic competition
c. Business cycle
d. Perfect competition

21. _____ or consumer demand or consumption is also known as personal consumption expenditure. It is the largest part of aggregate demand or effective demand at the macroeconomic level. There are two variants of consumption in the aggregate demand model, including induced consumption and autonomous consumption.

a. Value added
b. Consumer spending
c. Power III
d. Deregulation

22. _____ is income after subtracting taxes and normal expenses (such as rent or mortgage and food) to maintain a certain standard of living. It is the amount of an individual's income available for spending after the essentials (such as food, clothing, and shelter) have been taken care of:

_____ = Gross income - taxes - necessities

Despite the formal definitions above, disposable income is commonly used to denote _____. The meaning should therefore be interpreted from context.

Chapter 5. External Considerations in Marketing Introduction

a. 6-3-5 Brainwriting
b. 180SearchAssistant
c. Power III
d. Discretionary income

23. In economics, the term _____ describes the reduction of a country's gross domestic product (GDP) for at least two quarters. The usual dictionary definition is 'a period of reduced economic activity', a business cycle contraction.

The United States-based National Bureau of Economic Research (NBER) defines economic _____ as: 'a significant decline in [the] economic activity spread across the country, lasting more than a few months, normally visible in real GDP growth, real personal income, employment (non-farm payrolls), industrial production, and wholesale-retail sales.' The NBER's Business Cycle Dating Committee is generally seen as the authority for dating US _____s.

a. Macroeconomics
b. Leading indicator
c. Law of demand
d. Recession

24. _____ or _____ data refers to selected population characteristics as used in government, marketing or opinion research, or the _____ profiles used in such research. Note the distinction from the term 'demography' Commonly-used _____ include race, age, income, disabilities, mobility (in terms of travel time to work or number of vehicles available), educational attainment, home ownership, employment status, and even location.
a. African Americans
b. Albert Einstein
c. AStore
d. Demographic

25. The _____ is a model used to represent the process of explaining the transformation of countries from high birth rates and high death rates to low birth rates and low death rates as part of the economic development of a country from a pre-industrial to an industrialized economy. It is based on an interpretation begun in 1929 by the American demographer Warren Thompson of prior observed changes, or transitions, in birth and death rates in industrialized societies over the past two hundred years.

Most developed countries are beyond stage three of the model; the majority of developing countries are in stage 2 or stage 3.

a. 6-3-5 Brainwriting
b. Demographic transition model
c. Power III
d. 180SearchAssistant

26. _____ is difficult to define. For example, in 1952, Alfred Kroeber and Clyde Kluckhohn compiled a list of 164 definitions of '_____' in _____: A Critical Review of Concepts and Definitions. However, the word '_____' is most commonly used in three basic senses:

- excellence of taste in the fine arts and humanities
- an integrated pattern of human knowledge, belief, and behavior that depends upon the capacity for symbolic thought and social learning
- the set of shared attitudes, values, goals, and practices that characterizes an institution, organization or group.

When the concept first emerged in eighteenth- and nineteenth-century Europe, it connoted a process of cultivation or improvement, as in agriculture or horticulture. In the nineteenth century, it came to refer first to the betterment or refinement of the individual, especially through education, and then to the fulfillment of national aspirations or ideals.

a. Albert Einstein
b. African Americans
c. AStore
d. Culture

27. _____ is commonly defined as the amount of a company's or a person's income before all deductions or any taxpayer's income, except that which is specifically excluded by the Internal Revenue Code, before taking deductions or taxes into account. For a business, this amount is pre-tax net sales less cost of sales. Section 61 of the Internal Revenue Code (Code) defines '_____' as 'all income from whatever source derived.' Section 61(a) of the Code lists fifteen examples of items included in _____; however, the list is not exhaustive.

a. Power III
b. 6-3-5 Brainwriting
c. 180SearchAssistant
d. Gross income

28. In sociology, anthropology and cultural studies, a _____ is a group of people with a culture (whether distinct or hidden) which differentiates them from the larger culture to which they belong. If a particular _____ is characterized by a systematic opposition to the dominant culture, it may be described as a counterculture. As Ken Gelder notes, _____s are social, with their own shared conventions, values and rituals, but they can also seem 'immersed' or self-absorbed--another feature that distinguishes them from countercultures.

a. Power III
b. 180SearchAssistant
c. 6-3-5 Brainwriting
d. Subculture

29. _____ is an authority or agency in a country responsible for collecting and safeguarding _____ duties and for controlling the flow of goods including animals, personal effects and hazardous items in and out of a country. Depending on local legislation and regulations, the import or export of some goods may be restricted or forbidden, and the _____ agency enforces these rules. The _____ agency may be different from the immigration authority, which monitors persons who leave or enter the country, checking for appropriate documentation, apprehending people wanted by international arrest warrants, and impeding the entry of others deemed dangerous to the country.
    a. Specific Performance
    b. Registered trademark symbol
    c. Madrid system for the international registration of marks
    d. Customs

30. A personal and cultural _____ is a relative ethic _____, an assumption upon which implementation can be extrapolated. A _____ system is a set of consistent _____s and measures that is soo not true. A principle _____ is a foundation upon which other _____s and measures of integrity are based.
    a. Value
    b. Perceptual maps
    c. Supreme Court of the United States
    d. Package-on-Package

Chapter 6. Transitioning to Services Marketing

1. _____ is an advertisement in which a particular product specifically mentions a competitor by name for the express purpose of showing why the competitor is inferior to the product naming it.

This should not be confused with parody advertisements, where a fictional product is being advertised for the purpose of poking fun at the particular advertisement, nor should it be confused with the use of a coined brand name for the purpose of comparing the product without actually naming an actual competitor. ('Wikipedia tastes better and is less filling than the Encyclopedia Galactica.')

In the 1980s, during what has been referred to as the cola wars, soft-drink manufacturer Pepsi ran a series of advertisements where people, caught on hidden camera, in a blind taste test, chose Pepsi over rival Coca-Cola.

a. Cost per conversion
b. Comparative advertising
c. GL-70
d. Heavy-up

2. _____ is marketing based on relationship and value. It may be used to market a service or a product.

Marketing a service-base business is different from marketing a goods-base business.

a. Power III
b. 180SearchAssistant
c. 6-3-5 Brainwriting
d. Services marketing

3. Maslow's _____ is a theory in psychology, proposed by Abraham Maslow in his 1943 paper A Theory of Human Motivation, which he subsequently extended to include his observations of humans' innate curiosity.

Maslow studied what he called exemplary people such as Albert Einstein, Jane Addams, Eleanor Roosevelt, and Frederick Douglass rather than mentally ill or neurotic people, writing that 'the study of crippled, stunted, immature, and unhealthy specimens can yield only a cripple psychology and a cripple philosophy.' Maslow also studied the healthiest one percent of the college student population. In his book, The Farther Reaches of Human Nature, Maslow writes, 'By ordinary standards of this kind of laboratory research...

a. Hierarchy of needs
b. 6-3-5 Brainwriting
c. 180SearchAssistant
d. Power III

Chapter 6. Transitioning to Services Marketing

4. _____ is defined by the American _____ Association as the activity, set of institutions, and processes for creating, communicating, delivering, and exchanging offerings that have value for customers, clients, partners, and society at large. The term developed from the original meaning which referred literally to going to market, as in shopping, or going to a market to sell goods or services.

_____ practice tends to be seen as a creative industry, which includes advertising, distribution and selling.

   a. Customer acquisition management
   b. Marketing myopia
   c. Marketing
   d. Product naming

5. _____ is systematic determination of merit, worth, and significance of something or someone using criteria against a set of standards. _____ often is used to characterize and appraise subjects of interest in a wide range of human enterprises, including the arts, criminal justice, foundations and non-profit organizations, government, health care, and other human services.

Depending on the topic of interest, there are professional groups which look to the quality and rigor of the _____ process.

   a. ADTECH
   b. AMAX
   c. Evaluation
   d. ACNielsen

6. _____ is a term used to describe a person who was born during the demographic Post-World War II baby boom. Many analysts now believe that two distinct cultural generations were born during this baby boom; the older generation is often called the Baby Boom Generation and the younger generation is often called Generation Jones. The term '_____' is sometimes used in a cultural context, and sometimes used to describe someone who was born during the post-WWII baby boom.
   a. Greatest Generation
   b. Baby Boomer
   c. AStore
   d. Generation X

7. _____ is used in marketing to describe the inability to assess the value gained from engaging in an activity using any tangible evidence. It is often used to describe services where there isn't a tangible product that the customer can purchase, that can be seen, tasted or touched.

Other key characteristics of services include perishability, inseparability and variability.

a. Automated surveys
b. Individual branding
c. Inseparability
d. Intangibility

8. _____ is a broad label that refers to any individuals or households that use goods and services generated within the economy. The concept of a _____ is used in different contexts, so that the usage and significance of the term may vary.

A _____ is a person who uses any product or service.

a. 6-3-5 Brainwriting
b. Power III
c. 180SearchAssistant
d. Consumer

9. _____ is a list for goods and materials held available in stock by a business. It is also used for a list of the contents of a household and for a list for testamentary purposes of the possessions of someone who has died. In accounting _____ is considered an asset.
a. ADTECH
b. ACNielsen
c. Inventory
d. Ending Inventory

10. _____ refers to messages and related media used to communicate with a market. Those who practice advertising, branding, direct marketing, graphic design, marketing, packaging, promotion, publicity, sponsorship, public relations, sales, sales promotion and online marketing are termed marketing communicators, _____ managers, or more briefly as marcom managers.
a. Merchandise
b. Merchandising
c. Sales promotion
d. Marketing communication

11. _____ can be regarded as an outcome of mental processes (cognitive process) leading to the selection of a course of action among several alternatives. Every _____ process produces a final choice. The output can be an action or an opinion of choice.

a. 180SearchAssistant
b. 6-3-5 Brainwriting
c. Decision making
d. Power III

12. _____ is a form of communication that typically attempts to persuade potential customers to purchase or to consume more of a particular brand of product or service. 'While now central to the contemporary global economy and the reproduction of global production networks, it is only quite recently that _____ has been more than a marginal influence on patterns of sales and production. The formation of modern _____ was intimately bound up with the emergence of new forms of monopoly capitalism around the end of the 19th and beginning of the 20th century as one element in corporate strategies to create, organize and where possible control markets, especially for mass produced consumer goods.
   a. ACNielsen
   b. AMAX
   c. Advertising
   d. ADTECH

13. _____ is the set of reasons that determines one to engage in a particular behavior. The term is generally used for human _____ but, theoretically, it can be used to describe the causes for animal behavior as well
   a. Motivation
   b. Power III
   c. Role playing
   d. 180SearchAssistant

14. In economics, an externality or spillover of an economic transaction is an impact on a party that is not directly involved in the transaction. In such a case, prices do not reflect the full costs or benefits in production or consumption of a product or service. A positive impact is called an _____ benefit, while a negative impact is called an _____ cost.
   a. AMAX
   b. ACNielsen
   c. ADTECH
   d. External

15. _____ is the study of when, why, how, where and what people do or do not buy products. It blends elements from psychology, sociology, social psychology, anthropology and economics. It attempts to understand the buyer decision making process, both individually and in groups. It studies characteristics of individual consumers such as demographics and behavioural variables in an attempt to understand people's wants. It also tries to assess influences on the consumer from groups such as family, friends, reference groups, and society in general.

a. Communal marketing
b. Consumer confidence
c. Consumer behavior
d. Multidimensional scaling

16. The _____ is generally accepted as the use and specification of the four p's describing the strategic position of a product in the marketplace. One version of the origins of the _____ starts in 1948 when James Culliton said that a marketing decision should be a result of something similar to a recipe. This version continued in 1953 when Neil Borden, in his American Marketing Association presidential address, took the recipe idea one step further and coined the term 'Marketing-Mix'.
a. 180SearchAssistant
b. Power III
c. 6-3-5 Brainwriting
d. Marketing mix

Chapter 7. Decision Making by Target Markets and Stakeholders

1. _____ can be regarded as an outcome of mental processes (cognitive process) leading to the selection of a course of action among several alternatives. Every _____ process produces a final choice. The output can be an action or an opinion of choice.
   a. Power III
   b. Decision making
   c. 6-3-5 Brainwriting
   d. 180SearchAssistant

2. _____ is a broad label that refers to any individuals or households that use goods and services generated within the economy. The concept of a _____ is used in different contexts, so that the usage and significance of the term may vary.

   A _____ is a person who uses any product or service.

   a. Power III
   b. Consumer
   c. 6-3-5 Brainwriting
   d. 180SearchAssistant

3. _____ is the study of when, why, how, where and what people do or do not buy products. It blends elements from psychology, sociology, social psychology, anthropology and economics. It attempts to understand the buyer decision making process, both individually and in groups. It studies characteristics of individual consumers such as demographics and behavioural variables in an attempt to understand people's wants. It also tries to assess influences on the consumer from groups such as family, friends, reference groups, and society in general.
   a. Multidimensional scaling
   b. Consumer confidence
   c. Communal marketing
   d. Consumer behavior

4. In economics, an externality or spillover of an economic transaction is an impact on a party that is not directly involved in the transaction. In such a case, prices do not reflect the full costs or benefits in production or consumption of a product or service. A positive impact is called an _____ benefit, while a negative impact is called an _____ cost.
   a. ADTECH
   b. ACNielsen
   c. AMAX
   d. External

Chapter 7. Decision Making by Target Markets and Stakeholders

5. _____ or _____ data refers to selected population characteristics as used in government, marketing or opinion research, or the _____ profiles used in such research. Note the distinction from the term 'demography' Commonly-used _____ include race, age, income, disabilities, mobility (in terms of travel time to work or number of vehicles available), educational attainment, home ownership, employment status, and even location.

   a. Albert Einstein
   b. AStore
   c. African Americans
   d. Demographic

6. The _____ is a model used to represent the process of explaining the transformation of countries from high birth rates and high death rates to low birth rates and low death rates as part of the economic development of a country from a pre-industrial to an industrialized economy. It is based on an interpretation begun in 1929 by the American demographer Warren Thompson of prior observed changes, or transitions, in birth and death rates in industrialized societies over the past two hundred years.

Most developed countries are beyond stage three of the model; the majority of developing countries are in stage 2 or stage 3.

   a. Power III
   b. 6-3-5 Brainwriting
   c. Demographic transition model
   d. 180SearchAssistant

7. _____ is difficult to define. For example, in 1952, Alfred Kroeber and Clyde Kluckhohn compiled a list of 164 definitions of '_____' in _____: A Critical Review of Concepts and Definitions. However, the word '_____' is most commonly used in three basic senses:

   - excellence of taste in the fine arts and humanities
   - an integrated pattern of human knowledge, belief, and behavior that depends upon the capacity for symbolic thought and social learning
   - the set of shared attitudes, values, goals, and practices that characterizes an institution, organization or group.

When the concept first emerged in eighteenth- and nineteenth-century Europe, it connoted a process of cultivation or improvement, as in agriculture or horticulture. In the nineteenth century, it came to refer first to the betterment or refinement of the individual, especially through education, and then to the fulfillment of national aspirations or ideals.

Chapter 7. Decision Making by Target Markets and Stakeholders

   a. AStore
   b. African Americans
   c. Albert Einstein
   d. Culture

8. _____ is an authority or agency in a country responsible for collecting and safeguarding _____ duties and for controlling the flow of goods including animals, personal effects and hazardous items in and out of a country. Depending on local legislation and regulations, the import or export of some goods may be restricted or forbidden, and the _____ agency enforces these rules. The _____ agency may be different from the immigration authority, which monitors persons who leave or enter the country, checking for appropriate documentation, apprehending people wanted by international arrest warrants, and impeding the entry of others deemed dangerous to the country.
   a. Madrid system for the international registration of marks
   b. Customs
   c. Registered trademark symbol
   d. Specific Performance

9. _____ is defined by the American _____ Association as the activity, set of institutions, and processes for creating, communicating, delivering, and exchanging offerings that have value for customers, clients, partners, and society at large. The term developed from the original meaning which referred literally to going to market, as in shopping, or going to a market to sell goods or services.

_____ practice tends to be seen as a creative industry, which includes advertising, distribution and selling.

   a. Customer acquisition management
   b. Marketing myopia
   c. Product naming
   d. Marketing

10. A personal and cultural _____ is a relative ethic _____, an assumption upon which implementation can be extrapolated. A _____ system is a set of consistent _____s and measures that is soo not true. A principle _____ is a foundation upon which other _____s and measures of integrity are based.
   a. Value
   b. Perceptual maps
   c. Package-on-Package
   d. Supreme Court of the United States

11. _____ is a concept that arose out of the theory of two-step flow of communication propounded by Paul Lazarsfeld and Elihu Katz. This theory is one of several models that try to explain the diffusion of innovations, ideas, or commercial products.

The opinion leader is the agent who is an active media user and who interprets the meaning of media messages or content for lower-end media users.

   a. Intellectual property
   b. ACNielsen
   c. Elasticity
   d. Opinion leadership

12. A _____ is a sociological concept referring to a group to which an individual or another group is compared.

_____s are used in order to evaluate and determine the nature of a given individual or other group's characteristics and sociological attributes. It is the group to which the individual relates or aspires relate himself or self psychologically.

   a. Minority
   b. Reference group
   c. Power III
   d. Mociology

13. In operant conditioning, _____ occurs when an event following a response causes an increase in the probability of that response occurring in the future. Response strength can be assessed by measures such as the frequency with which the response is made (for example, a pigeon may peck a key more times in the session), or the speed with which it is made (for example, a rat may run a maze faster.) The environment change contingent upon the response is called a reinforcer.
   a. Generic brands
   b. Relationship Management Application
   c. Completely randomized designs
   d. Reinforcement

14. In statistics, an _____ is a term in a statistical model added when the effect of two or more variables is not simply additive. Such a term reflects that the effect of one variable depends on the values of one or more other variables.

Thus, for a response Y and two variables x_1 and x_2 an additive model would be:

$$Y = ax_1 + bx_2 + \text{error}$$

In contrast to this,

$$Y = ax_1 + bx_2 + c(x_1 \times x_2) + \text{error},$$

is an example of a model with an _____ between variables x_1 and x_2 ('error' refers to the random variable whose value by which y differs from the expected value of y.)

a. AMAX
b. Interaction
c. ACNielsen
d. ADTECH

15. _____ is the set of reasons that determines one to engage in a particular behavior. The term is generally used for human _____ but, theoretically, it can be used to describe the causes for animal behavior as well

a. Power III
b. Role playing
c. 180SearchAssistant
d. Motivation

16. Maslow's _____ is a theory in psychology, proposed by Abraham Maslow in his 1943 paper A Theory of Human Motivation, which he subsequently extended to include his observations of humans' innate curiosity.

Maslow studied what he called exemplary people such as Albert Einstein, Jane Addams, Eleanor Roosevelt, and Frederick Douglass rather than mentally ill or neurotic people, writing that 'the study of crippled, stunted, immature, and unhealthy specimens can yield only a cripple psychology and a cripple philosophy.' Maslow also studied the healthiest one percent of the college student population. In his book, The Farther Reaches of Human Nature, Maslow writes, 'By ordinary standards of this kind of laboratory research...

a. 180SearchAssistant
b. Power III
c. 6-3-5 Brainwriting
d. Hierarchy of needs

17. _____ was originally coined by Austrian psychologist Alfred Adler in 1929. The current broader sense of the word dates from 1961.

In sociology, a _____ is the way a person lives.

a. 6-3-5 Brainwriting
b. 180SearchAssistant
c. Power III
d. Lifestyle

18. In the art of selling, _____ is one stage in a seven stage personal selling process.

In this stage the salesperson takes a qualified prospect through a series of question and answer sessions in order to identify the requirements of the prospect. During this step, the salesperson will attempt to help the buyer identify and quantify a business need or a 'gap' between where the client is today and where they would like to be in the future.

a. Power III
b. Product churning
c. 180SearchAssistant
d. Need identification

19. In psychology, philosophy, and the cognitive sciences, _____ is the process of attaining awareness or understanding of sensory information. It is a task far more complex than was imagined in the 1950s and 1960s, when it was predicted that building perceiving machines would take about a decade, a goal which is still very far from fruition. The word _____ comes from the Latin words _____, percepio, meaning 'receiving, collecting, action of taking possession, apprehension with the mind or senses.'

_____ is one of the oldest fields in psychology.

a. Perception
b. Groupthink
c. 180SearchAssistant
d. Power III

20. Cognition is the scientific term for 'the process of thought.' Its usage varies in different ways in accord with different disciplines: For example, in psychology and _____ science it refers to an information processing view of an individual's psychological functions. Other interpretations of the meaning of cognition link it to the development of concepts; individual minds, groups, organizations, and even larger coalitions of entities, can be modelled as 'societies' (Society of Mind), which cooperate to form concepts.

The autonomous elements of each 'society' would have the opportunity to demonstrate emergent behavior in the face of some crisis or opportunity.

Chapter 7. Decision Making by Target Markets and Stakeholders

   a. 180SearchAssistant
   b. Power III
   c. 6-3-5 Brainwriting
   d. Cognitive

21. _____ is an uncomfortable feeling caused by holding two contradictory ideas simultaneously. The 'ideas' or 'cognitions' in question may include attitudes and beliefs, and also the awareness of one's behavior. The theory of _____ proposes that people have a motivational drive to reduce dissonance by changing their attitudes, beliefs, and behaviors, or by justifying or rationalizing their attitudes, beliefs, and behaviors.
   a. 180SearchAssistant
   b. Power III
   c. Perception
   d. Cognitive dissonance

22. _____ is an advertisement in which a particular product specifically mentions a competitor by name for the express purpose of showing why the competitor is inferior to the product naming it.

This should not be confused with parody advertisements, where a fictional product is being advertised for the purpose of poking fun at the particular advertisement, nor should it be confused with the use of a coined brand name for the purpose of comparing the product without actually naming an actual competitor. ('Wikipedia tastes better and is less filling than the Encyclopedia Galactica.')

In the 1980s, during what has been referred to as the cola wars, soft-drink manufacturer Pepsi ran a series of advertisements where people, caught on hidden camera, in a blind taste test, chose Pepsi over rival Coca-Cola.

   a. Cost per conversion
   b. GL-70
   c. Heavy-up
   d. Comparative advertising

23. _____ is systematic determination of merit, worth, and significance of something or someone using criteria against a set of standards. _____ often is used to characterize and appraise subjects of interest in a wide range of human enterprises, including the arts, criminal justice, foundations and non-profit organizations, government, health care, and other human services.

Depending on the topic of interest, there are professional groups which look to the quality and rigor of the _____ process.

a. AMAX
b. ADTECH
c. Evaluation
d. ACNielsen

Chapter 8. Creating and Managing Products

1. A _____ is a collection of symbols, experiences and associations connected with a product, a service, a person or any other artifact or entity.

   _____s have become increasingly important components of culture and the economy, now being described as 'cultural accessories and personal philosophies'.

   Some people distinguish the psychological aspect of a _____ from the experiential aspect.

   a. Brand equity
   b. Store brand
   c. Brandable software
   d. Brand

2. _____ is an advertisement in which a particular product specifically mentions a competitor by name for the express purpose of showing why the competitor is inferior to the product naming it.

   This should not be confused with parody advertisements, where a fictional product is being advertised for the purpose of poking fun at the particular advertisement, nor should it be confused with the use of a coined brand name for the purpose of comparing the product without actually naming an actual competitor. ('Wikipedia tastes better and is less filling than the Encyclopedia Galactica.')

   In the 1980s, during what has been referred to as the cola wars, soft-drink manufacturer Pepsi ran a series of advertisements where people, caught on hidden camera, in a blind taste test, chose Pepsi over rival Coca-Cola.

   a. Cost per conversion
   b. Comparative advertising
   c. Heavy-up
   d. GL-70

3. A personal and cultural _____ is a relative ethic _____, an assumption upon which implementation can be extrapolated. A _____ system is a set of consistent _____s and measures that is soo not true. A principle _____ is a foundation upon which other _____s and measures of integrity are based.
   a. Perceptual maps
   b. Supreme Court of the United States
   c. Package-on-Package
   d. Value

4. The _____ is a professional association for marketers. As of 2008 it had approximately 40,000 members. There are collegiate chapters on 250 campuses.

a. AMAX
b. American Marketing Association
c. ADTECH
d. ACNielsen

5. _____ is defined by the American _____ Association as the activity, set of institutions, and processes for creating, communicating, delivering, and exchanging offerings that have value for customers, clients, partners, and society at large. The term developed from the original meaning which referred literally to going to market, as in shopping, or going to a market to sell goods or services.

_____ practice tends to be seen as a creative industry, which includes advertising, distribution and selling.

a. Marketing
b. Customer acquisition management
c. Marketing myopia
d. Product naming

6. In marketing, a _____ is a generic product augmented by everything that is needed for the customer to have a compelling reason to buy. The generic product is what is usually shipped to the customer. The _____ typically augments the generic product with training and support, manuals, cables, additional software or hardware, installation instructions, professional services, etc.
a. Jobbing house
b. Mass market
c. Teaser rate
d. Whole product

7. _____ in organizations and public policy is both the organizational process of creating and maintaining a plan; and the psychological process of thinking about the activities required to create a desired goal on some scale. As such, it is a fundamental property of intelligent behavior. This thought process is essential to the creation and refinement of a plan, or integration of it with other plans, that is, it combines forecasting of developments with the preparation of scenarios of how to react to them.
a. Power III
b. Planning
c. 6-3-5 Brainwriting
d. 180SearchAssistant

8. _____ is the ongoing process of identifying and articulating market requirements that define a product's feature set.

Chapter 8. Creating and Managing Products

a. Product planning
b. Market intelligence
c. Brand parity
d. Targeted advertising

9. A _____ is a plan of action designed to achieve a particular goal.

_____ is different from tactics. In military terms, tactics is concerned with the conduct of an engagement while _____ is concerned with how different engagements are linked.

a. 180SearchAssistant
b. Strategy
c. Power III
d. 6-3-5 Brainwriting

10. _____, in strategic management and marketing, is the percentage or proportion of the total available market or market segment that is being serviced by a company. It can be expressed as a company's sales revenue (from that market) divided by the total sales revenue available in that market. It can also be expressed as a company's unit sales volume (in a market) divided by the total volume of units sold in that market.

a. Customer relationship management
b. Cyberdoc
c. Market share
d. Demand generation

11. In business and engineering, new _____ is the term used to describe the complete process of bringing a new product or service to market. There are two parallel paths involved in the Nproduct development process: one involves the idea generation, product design, and detail engineering; the other involves market research and marketing analysis. Companies typically see new _____ as the first stage in generating and commercializing new products within the overall strategic process of product life cycle management used to maintain or grow their market share.

a. New product development
b. Specification tree
c. Product development
d. New product screening

12. Competitiveness is a comparative concept of the ability and performance of a firm, sub-sector or country to sell and supply goods and/or services in a given market. Although widely used in economics and business management, the usefulness of the concept, particularly in the context of national competitiveness, is vigorously disputed by economists, such as Paul Krugman .

Chapter 8. Creating and Managing Products 59

The term may also be applied to markets, where it is used to refer to the extent to which the market structure may be regarded as perfectly _____.

  a. Customs union
  b. Geographical pricing
  c. Free trade zone
  d. Competitive

13. _____ can be regarded as an outcome of mental processes (cognitive process) leading to the selection of a course of action among several alternatives. Every _____ process produces a final choice. The output can be an action or an opinion of choice.
  a. 6-3-5 Brainwriting
  b. 180SearchAssistant
  c. Power III
  d. Decision making

14. A _____ or trade mark, identified by the symbols ™ (not yet registered) and ® (registered) business organization or other legal entity to identify that the products and/or services to consumers with which the _____ appears originate from a unique source of origin, and to distinguish its products or services from those of other entities. A _____ is a type of intellectual property, and typically a name, word, phrase, logo, symbol, design, image, or a combination of these elements. There is also a range of non-conventional _____s comprising marks which do not fall into these standard categories.
  a. 180SearchAssistant
  b. Power III
  c. Risk management
  d. Trademark

15. _____ is one of the four elements of marketing mix. An organization or set of organizations (go-betweens) involved in the process of making a product or service available for use or consumption by a consumer or business user.

The other three parts of the marketing mix are product, pricing, and promotion.

  a. Comparison-Shopping agent
  b. Better Living Through Chemistry
  c. Japan Advertising Photographers' Association
  d. Distribution

Chapter 8. Creating and Managing Products

16. _____ is systematic determination of merit, worth, and significance of something or someone using criteria against a set of standards. _____ often is used to characterize and appraise subjects of interest in a wide range of human enterprises, including the arts, criminal justice, foundations and non-profit organizations, government, health care, and other human services.

Depending on the topic of interest, there are professional groups which look to the quality and rigor of the _____ process.

a. AMAX
b. ACNielsen
c. ADTECH
d. Evaluation

17. _____ is a service provided by many retailers of various products, primarily electronics, that provides the end-user with a resource for information regarding the product, and help if the product should malfunction. _____ can be found in most manuals for products in the form of a phone number, website address, or physical location.

The Internet has allowed for a new form of _____ to develop.

a. Psychological pricing
b. Price-weighted
c. Product life cycle
d. Product support

18. A product _____ is the use of an established product's brand name for a new item in the same product category. _____s occur when a company introduces additional items in the same product category under the same brand name such as new flavors, forms, colors, added ingredients, package sizes.Examples includei) Zen LXI, Zen VXIii) Surf, Surf Excel, Surf Excel Blueiii) Splendour, Splendour Plusiv) Coke, Diet Coke, Vanilla Cokev) Clinic All Clear, Clinic Plus

- brand
- brand management
- marketing
- product management
- Product lining

a. Brand Development Index
b. Line extension
c. Perishability
d. Targeted advertising

Chapter 8. Creating and Managing Products

19. A _____ is the use of an established product's brand name for a new item in the same product category. _____s occur when a company introduces additional items in the same product category under the same brand name such as new flavors, forms, colors, added ingredients, package sizes.
    a. Retail floor planning
    b. Pearson's chi-square
    c. Comparison-Shopping agent
    d. Product line extension

20. There are many important decisions about product and service development and marketing. In the process of product development and marketing we should focus on strategic decisions about product attributes, product branding, product packaging, product labeling and product support services. But product strategy also calls for building a _____.
    a. Macromarketing
    b. Technology acceptance model
    c. Pinstorm
    d. Product line

21. _____ or brand stretching is a marketing strategy in which a firm marketing a product with a well-developed image uses the same brand name in a different product category. Organizations use this strategy to increase and leverage brand equity (definition: the net worth and long-term sustainability just from the renowned name.) An example of a _____ is Jello-gelatin creating Jello pudding pops.
    a. Brand extension
    b. Web 2.0
    c. Brand orientation
    d. Brand awareness

22. _____ is when a large distribution channel member (usually a retailer), buys from a manufacturer in bulk and puts its own name on the product. This strategy is only practical when the retailer does very high levels of volume. The advantages to the retailer are:

  - more freedom and flexibility in pricing
  - more control over product attributes and quality
  - higher margins (or lower selling price)
  - eliminates much of the manufacturer's promotional costs

Chapter 8. Creating and Managing Products

The advantages to the manufacturer are:

- reduced promotional costs
- stability of sales volume (at least while the contract is operative)

- Kumar, Nirmalya; Steenkamp, Jan-Benedict E.M., Private Label Strategy - How to Meet the Store Brand Challenge. Harvard Business Press 2007

- private label
- brand management
- brand
- product management
- marketing

a. Rural market
b. Customization
c. Promotion
d. Private branding

23. _____ occurs when organizations market many variations of the same products. This can be done through different colour combinations, product sizes and different product uses. This produces diversity for the firm as it is able to capture its sizeable portion of the market.
   a. Hoarding
   b. Marginal revenue
   c. Total cost
   d. Product proliferation

24. _____ is a broad label that refers to any individuals or households that use goods and services generated within the economy. The concept of a _____ is used in different contexts, so that the usage and significance of the term may vary.

A _____ is a person who uses any product or service.

   a. 180SearchAssistant
   b. Power III
   c. Consumer
   d. 6-3-5 Brainwriting

Chapter 8. Creating and Managing Products

25. The _____ is generally accepted as the use and specification of the four p's describing the strategic position of a product in the marketplace. One version of the origins of the _____ starts in 1948 when James Culliton said that a marketing decision should be a result of something similar to a recipe. This version continued in 1953 when Neil Borden, in his American Marketing Association presidential address, took the recipe idea one step further and coined the term 'Marketing-Mix'.
    a. 6-3-5 Brainwriting
    b. 180SearchAssistant
    c. Power III
    d. Marketing mix

26. _____, fundamental research (sometimes pure research), is research carried out to increase understanding of fundamental principles. Many times the end results have no direct or immediate commercial benefits, which is to say that _____ can be thought of as arising out of pure curiosity. However, in the long term it is the basis for many commercial products and applied research.
    a. Power III
    b. Response rate
    c. Reference value
    d. Basic research

27. In marketing, _____ is the process of distinguishing the differences of a product or offering from others, to make it more attractive to a particular target market. This involves differentiating it from competitors' products as well as one's own product offerings.

    Differentiation is a source of competitive advantage.

    a. Packshot
    b. Corporate image
    c. Marketing myopia
    d. Product differentiation

28. The phrase _____ refers to the aspect of corporate strategy, corporate finance and management dealing with the buying, selling and combining of different companies that can aid, finance, or help a growing company in a given industry grow rapidly without having to create another business entity.

    An acquisition, also known as a takeover or a buyout, is the buying of one company (the 'target') by another. An acquisition may be friendly or hostile.

a. Power III
b. 6-3-5 Brainwriting
c. 180SearchAssistant
d. Mergers and acquisitions

29. In economics, an externality or spillover of an economic transaction is an impact on a party that is not directly involved in the transaction. In such a case, prices do not reflect the full costs or benefits in production or consumption of a product or service. A positive impact is called an _____ benefit, while a negative impact is called an _____ cost.
   a. ADTECH
   b. External
   c. AMAX
   d. ACNielsen

30. A _____ is an entity formed between two or more parties to undertake economic activity together. The parties agree to create a new entity by both contributing equity, and they then share in the revenues, expenses, and control of the enterprise. The venture can be for one specific project only, or a continuing business relationship such as the Fuji Xerox _____.
   a. Gripe site
   b. Joint venture
   c. Trademark attorney
   d. Consumer protection

31. The verb _____ or grant _____ means to give permission. The noun _____ refers to that permission as well as to the document memorializing that permission. _____ may be granted by a party to another party as an element of an agreement between those parties.
   a. Power III
   b. 6-3-5 Brainwriting
   c. 180SearchAssistant
   d. License

32. A _____ is a set of exclusive rights granted by a State to an inventor or his assignee for a limited period of time in exchange for a disclosure of an invention.

The procedure for granting _____s, the requirements placed on the _____ee and the extent of the exclusive rights vary widely between countries according to national laws and international agreements. Typically, however, a _____ application must include one or more claims defining the invention which must be new, inventive, and useful or industrially applicable.

Chapter 8. Creating and Managing Products

a. Reasonable person standard
b. Foreign Corrupt Practices Act
c. Product liability
d. Patent

33. In business and engineering, _____ is the term used to describe the complete process of bringing a new product or service to market. There are two parallel paths involved in the _____ process: one involves the idea generation, product design, and detail engineering; the other involves market research and marketing analysis. Companies typically see _____ as the first stage in generating and commercializing new products within the overall strategic process of product life cycle management used to maintain or grow their market share.
    a. Product optimization
    b. Product development
    c. New product development
    d. Specification

34. A _____ is a company or individual that purchases goods or services with the intention of reselling them rather than consuming or using them. This is usually done for profit (but could be resold at a loss.) One example can be found in the industry of telecommunications, where companies buy excess amounts of transmission capacity or call time from other carriers and resell it to smaller carriers.
    a. Discontinuation
    b. Jobbing house
    c. Reseller
    d. Value-based pricing

35. _____ is the set of tasks, knowledge, and techniques required to identify business needs and determine solutions to business problems. Solutions often include a systems development component, but may also consist of process improvement or organizational change. The person who carries out this task is called a business analyst or _____.
    a. Business analysis
    b. Fast moving consumer goods
    c. Marketing management
    d. Door-to-door

Chapter 8. Creating and Managing Products

36. A _____, in the field of business and marketing, is a geographic region or demographic group used to gauge the viability of a product or service in the mass market prior to a wide scale roll-out. The criteria used to judge the acceptability of a _____ region or group include:

  1. a population that is demographically similar to the proposed target market; and
  2. relative isolation from densely populated media markets so that advertising to the test audience can be efficient and economical.

The _____ ideally aims to duplicate 'everything' - promotion and distribution as well as `product' - on a smaller scale. The technique replicates, typically in one area, what is planned to occur in a national launch; and the results are very carefully monitored, so that they can be extrapolated to projected national results. The `area' may be any one of the following:

- Television area
- Test town
- Residential neighborhood
- Test site

A number of decisions have to be taken about any _____:

- Which _____?
- What is to be tested?
- How long a test?
- What are the success criteria?

The simple go or no-go decision, together with the related reduction of risk, is normally the main justification for the expense of _____s. At the same time, however, such _____s can be used to test specific elements of a new product's marketing mix; possibly the version of the product itself, the promotional message and media spend, the distribution channels and the price.

 a. 180SearchAssistant
 b. Test market
 c. Power III
 d. Preadolescence

37. _____ is the process or cycle of introducing a new product into the market. The actual launch of a new product is the final stage of new product development, and the one where the most money will have to be spent for advertising, sales promotion, and other marketing efforts. In the case of a new consumer packaged good, costs will be at least $ 10 million, but can reach up to $ 200 million.

a. Customer Interaction Tracker
b. Confusion marketing
c. Sweepstakes
d. Commercialization

38. Cognition is the scientific term for 'the process of thought.' Its usage varies in different ways in accord with different disciplines: For example, in psychology and _____ science it refers to an information processing view of an individual's psychological functions. Other interpretations of the meaning of cognition link it to the development of concepts; individual minds, groups, organizations, and even larger coalitions of entities, can be modelled as 'societies' (Society of Mind), which cooperate to form concepts.

The autonomous elements of each 'society' would have the opportunity to demonstrate emergent behavior in the face of some crisis or opportunity.

a. 6-3-5 Brainwriting
b. Power III
c. 180SearchAssistant
d. Cognitive

Chapter 9. Communicating to Mass Markets

1. _____ is one of the four Ps of the marketing mix. The other three aspects are product, promotion, and place. It is also a key variable in microeconomic price allocation theory.
   a. Price
   b. Relationship based pricing
   c. Competitor indexing
   d. Pricing

2. _____ , according to The American Marketing Association, is 'a planning process designed to assure that all brand contacts received by a customer or prospect for a product, service, or organization are relevant to that person and consistent over time.' (Marketing Power Dictionary)

   _____ is a term used to describe a holistic approach to marketing. It aims to ensure consistency of message and the complementary use of media. The concept includes online and offline marketing channels.

   a. AMAX
   b. ADTECH
   c. ACNielsen
   d. Integrated marketing communications

3. _____ is one of the four aspects of promotional mix. (The other three parts of the promotional mix are advertising, personal selling, and publicity/public relations.) Media and non-media marketing communication are employed for a pre-determined, limited time to increase consumer demand, stimulate market demand or improve product availability.
   a. New Media Strategies
   b. Merchandise
   c. Sales promotion
   d. Marketing communication

4. In marketing and advertising, a _____ usually an advertising campaign, is aimed at appealing to. A _____ can be people of a certain age group, gender, marital status, etc. (ex: teenagers, females, single people, etc.)
   a. Targeted advertising
   b. Brand Development Index
   c. National brand
   d. Target audience

5. _____ is a business term meaning the market segment to which a particular good or service is marketed. It is mainly defined by age, gender, geography, socio-economic grouping, technographic, or any other combination of demographics. It is generally studied and mapped by an organization through lists and reports containing demographic information that may have an effect on the marketing of key products or services.

Chapter 9. Communicating to Mass Markets

a. Brando
b. Category Development Index
c. Distribution
d. Market specialization

6. _____ is defined by the American _____ Association as the activity, set of institutions, and processes for creating, communicating, delivering, and exchanging offerings that have value for customers, clients, partners, and society at large. The term developed from the original meaning which referred literally to going to market, as in shopping, or going to a market to sell goods or services.

_____ practice tends to be seen as a creative industry, which includes advertising, distribution and selling.

a. Marketing
b. Customer acquisition management
c. Product naming
d. Marketing myopia

7. _____ involves disseminating information about a product, product line, brand, or company. It is one of the four key aspects of the marketing mix. (The other three elements are product marketing, pricing, and distribution). P>_____ is generally sub-divided into two parts:

- Above the line _____: Promotion in the media (e.g. TV, radio, newspapers, Internet and Mobile Phones) in which the advertiser pays an advertising agency to place the ad
- Below the line _____: All other _____. Much of this is intended to be subtle enough for the consumer to be unaware that _____ is taking place. E.g. sponsorship, product placement, endorsements, sales _____, merchandising, direct mail, personal selling, public relations, trade shows

a. Cashmere Agency
b. Promotion
c. Davie Brown Index
d. Bottling lines

8. _____ is a form of communication that typically attempts to persuade potential customers to purchase or to consume more of a particular brand of product or service. 'While now central to the contemporary global economy and the reproduction of global production networks, it is only quite recently that _____ has been more than a marginal influence on patterns of sales and production. The formation of modern _____ was intimately bound up with the emergence of new forms of monopoly capitalism around the end of the 19th and beginning of the 20th century as one element in corporate strategies to create, organize and where possible control markets, especially for mass produced consumer goods.

Chapter 9. Communicating to Mass Markets

   a. ACNielsen
   b. ADTECH
   c. AMAX
   d. Advertising

9. _____ is a sales technique in which a salesperson walks from one door of a house to another trying to sell a product or service to the general public. A variant of this involves cold calling first, when another sales representative attempts to gain agreement that a salesperson should visit. _____ selling is usually conducted in the afternoon hours, when the majority of people are at home.
   a. Door-to-door
   b. Performance-based advertising
   c. Fast moving consumer goods
   d. Marketing management

10. _____ refers to messages and related media used to communicate with a market. Those who practice advertising, branding, direct marketing, graphic design, marketing, packaging, promotion, publicity, sponsorship, public relations, sales, sales promotion and online marketing are termed marketing communicators, _____ managers, or more briefly as marcom managers.
   a. Sales promotion
   b. Marketing Communication
   c. Merchandise
   d. Merchandising

11. _____ is the practice of managing the flow of information between an organization and its publics. _____ - often referred to as _____ - gains an organization or individual exposure to their audiences using topics of public interest and news items that do not require direct payment. Because _____ places exposure in credible third-party outlets, it offers a third-party legitimacy that advertising does not have.
   a. Graphic communication
   b. Power III
   c. Symbolic analysis
   d. Public relations

12. A _____ is a plan of action designed to achieve a particular goal.

_____ is different from tactics. In military terms, tactics is concerned with the conduct of an engagement while _____ is concerned with how different engagements are linked.

a. 6-3-5 Brainwriting
b. Power III
c. Strategy
d. 180SearchAssistant

13. Advertising mail junk mail is the delivery of advertising material to recipients of postal mail. The delivery of advertising mail forms a large and growing service for many postal services, and _____ marketing forms a significant portion of the direct marketing industry. Some organizations attempt to help people opt-out of receiving advertising mail, in many cases motivated by a concern over its negative environmental impact.
   a. Phishing
   b. Directory Harvest Attack
   c. Telemarketing
   d. Direct mail

14. _____ refers to the evolving trend in marketing whereby marketing has moved from a transaction-based effort to a conversation. The definition of _____ comes from John Deighton at Harvard, who says _____ is the ability to address the customer, remember what the customer says and address the customer again in a way that illustrates that we remember what the customer has told us (Deighton 1996.) _____ is not synonymous with online marketing, although _____ processes are facilitated by internet technology.
   a. InfoNU
   b. Outsourcing relationship management
   c. European Information Technology Observatory
   d. Interactive marketing

15. _____ is a market coverage strategy in which a firm decides to ignore market segment differences and go after the whole market with one offer.it is type of marketing (or attempting to sell through persuasion) of a product to a wide audience. The idea is to broadcast a message that will reach the largest number of people possible. Traditionally _____ has focused on radio, television and newspapers as the medium used to reach this broad audience.
   a. Business-to-consumer
   b. Mass marketing
   c. Marketspace
   d. Cyberdoc

Chapter 9. Communicating to Mass Markets

16. _____ is a term used to denote a section of the media specifically designed to reach a very large audience such as the population of a nation state. It was coined in the 1920s with the advent of nationwide radio networks, mass-circulation newspapers and magazines, although _____ were present centuries before the term became common. The term public media has a similar meaning: it is the sum of the public mass distributors of news and entertainment across media such as newspapers, television, radio, broadcasting, which may require union membership in some large markets such as Newspaper Guild, AFTRA, ' text publishers.
    a. 180SearchAssistant
    b. Mass media
    c. Power III
    d. 6-3-5 Brainwriting

17. _____ generally refers to a list of all planned expenses and revenues. It is a plan for saving and spending. A _____ is an important concept in microeconomics, which uses a _____ line to illustrate the trade-offs between two or more goods.
    a. Power III
    b. 180SearchAssistant
    c. 6-3-5 Brainwriting
    d. Budget

18. The _____ is a professional association for marketers. As of 2008 it had approximately 40,000 members. There are collegiate chapters on 250 campuses.
    a. ACNielsen
    b. American Marketing Association
    c. AMAX
    d. ADTECH

19. In economics, business, retail, and accounting, a _____ is the value of money that has been used up to produce something, and hence is not available for use anymore. In economics, a _____ is an alternative that is given up as a result of a decision. In business, the _____ may be one of acquisition, in which case the amount of money expended to acquire it is counted as _____.
    a. Fixed costs
    b. Transaction cost
    c. Variable cost
    d. Cost

20. In economics, an externality or spillover of an economic transaction is an impact on a party that is not directly involved in the transaction. In such a case, prices do not reflect the full costs or benefits in production or consumption of a product or service. A positive impact is called an _____ benefit, while a negative impact is called an _____ cost.

Chapter 9. Communicating to Mass Markets

a. ACNielsen
b. External
c. ADTECH
d. AMAX

21. _____ is a measure of the strength of a brand, product, service relative to competitive offerings. There is often a geographic element to the competitive landscape. In defining _____, you must see to what extent a product, brand, or firm controls a product category in a given geographic area.

a. Market dominance
b. Market system
c. Productivity
d. Discretionary spending

22. A _____ or pamphlet is a leaflet advertisement. _____s may advertise locations, events, hotels, products, services, etc. They are usually succinct in language and eye-catching in design.

a. Sweepstakes
b. Customer relationship management
c. Marketspace
d. Brochure

23. _____ is the physical search for minerals, fossils, precious metals or mineral specimens, and is also known as fossicking.

_____ is synonymous in some ways with mineral exploration which is an organised, large scale and at least semi-scientific effort undertaken by mineral resource companies to find commercially viable ore deposits. To actually be considered a prospector you must become registered as a professional prospector.

a. 6-3-5 Brainwriting
b. 180SearchAssistant
c. Power III
d. Prospecting

24. _____ in organizations and public policy is both the organizational process of creating and maintaining a plan; and the psychological process of thinking about the activities required to create a desired goal on some scale. As such, it is a fundamental property of intelligent behavior. This thought process is essential to the creation and refinement of a plan, or integration of it with other plans, that is, it combines forecasting of developments with the preparation of scenarios of how to react to them.

a. Power III
b. Planning
c. 6-3-5 Brainwriting
d. 180SearchAssistant

Chapter 10. Pricing The Product

1. _____ is one of the four Ps of the marketing mix. The other three aspects are product, promotion, and place. It is also a key variable in microeconomic price allocation theory.
   a. Relationship based pricing
   b. Price
   c. Competitor indexing
   d. Pricing

2. A personal and cultural _____ is a relative ethic _____, an assumption upon which implementation can be extrapolated. A _____ system is a set of consistent _____s and measures that is soo not true. A principle _____ is a foundation upon which other _____s and measures of integrity are based.
   a. Package-on-Package
   b. Perceptual maps
   c. Supreme Court of the United States
   d. Value

3. _____ refers to the additional value of a commodity over the cost of commodities used to produce it from the previous stage of production. An example is the price of gasoline at the pump over the price of the oil in it. In national accounts used in macroeconomics, it refers to the contribution of the factors of production, i.e., land, labor, and capital goods, to raising the value of a product and corresponds to the incomes received by the owners of these factors. The factors of production provide 'services' which raise the unit price of a product (X) relative to the cost per unit of intermediate goods used up in the production of X. _____ is shared between the factors of production (capital, labor, also human capital), giving rise to issues of distribution.
   a. Deregulation
   b. Power III
   c. Consumer spending
   d. Value added

4. _____ or goals give direction to the whole pricing process. Determining what your objectives are is the first step in pricing. When deciding on _____ you must consider: 1) the overall financial, marketing, and strategic objectives of the company; 2) the objectives of your product or brand; 3) consumer price elasticity and price points; and 4) the resources you have available.
   a. Transfer pricing
   b. Competitor indexing
   c. Discounts and allowances
   d. Pricing objectives

Chapter 10. Pricing The Product

5. _____, in strategic management and marketing, is the percentage or proportion of the total available market or market segment that is being serviced by a company. It can be expressed as a company's sales revenue (from that market) divided by the total sales revenue available in that market. It can also be expressed as a company's unit sales volume (in a market) divided by the total volume of units sold in that market.
   a. Customer relationship management
   b. Demand generation
   c. Cyberdoc
   d. Market share

6. _____ is a rivalry between individuals, groups, nations for territory, a niche, or allocation of resources. It arises whenever two or more parties strive for a goal which cannot be shared. _____ occurs naturally between living organisms which co-exist in the same environment.
   a. Price competition
   b. Price fixing
   c. Non-price competition
   d. Competition

7. Competitiveness is a comparative concept of the ability and performance of a firm, sub-sector or country to sell and supply goods and/or services in a given market. Although widely used in economics and business management, the usefulness of the concept, particularly in the context of national competitiveness, is vigorously disputed by economists, such as Paul Krugman .

The term may also be applied to markets, where it is used to refer to the extent to which the market structure may be regarded as perfectly _____.

   a. Competitive
   b. Free trade zone
   c. Geographical pricing
   d. Customs union

8. _____ is a marketing strategy 'in which one firm tries to distinguish its product or service from competing products on the basis of attributes like design and workmanship' (McConnell-Brue, 2002, p. 437-438.) The firm can also distinguish its product offering through quality of service, extensive distribution, customer focus, or any other sustainable competitive advantage other than price.
   a. Direct competition
   b. Price competition
   c. Non-price competition
   d. Price fixing

Chapter 10. Pricing The Product

9. _____ is defined by the American _____ Association as the activity, set of institutions, and processes for creating, communicating, delivering, and exchanging offerings that have value for customers, clients, partners, and society at large. The term developed from the original meaning which referred literally to going to market, as in shopping, or going to a market to sell goods or services.

_____ practice tends to be seen as a creative industry, which includes advertising, distribution and selling.

   a. Marketing myopia
   b. Product naming
   c. Customer acquisition management
   d. Marketing

10. _____ is a broad label that refers to any individuals or households that use goods and services generated within the economy. The concept of a _____ is used in different contexts, so that the usage and significance of the term may vary.

A _____ is a person who uses any product or service.

   a. 6-3-5 Brainwriting
   b. 180SearchAssistant
   c. Power III
   d. Consumer

11. _____ is an American magazine published monthly by Consumers Union. It publishes reviews and comparisons of consumer products and services based on reporting and results from its in-house testing laboratory. It also publishes cleaning and general buying guides.
   a. Magalog
   b. Consumer Reports
   c. Crossing the Chasm
   d. Power III

12. _____ in economics and business is the result of an exchange and from that trade we assign a numerical monetary value to a good, service or asset. If I trade 4 apples for an orange, the _____ of an orange is 4 - apples. Inversely, the _____ of an apple is 1/4 oranges.
   a. Pricing
   b. Contribution margin-based pricing
   c. Price
   d. Discounts and allowances

13. _____ is a term used in business to indicate a state of intense competitive rivalry accompanied by a multi-lateral series of price reduction. One competitor will lower its price, then others will lower their prices to match. If one of them reduces their price again, a new round of reductions starts.

   a. Pricing objectives
   b. Competitor indexing
   c. Resale price maintenance
   d. Price war

14. A _____ is a plan of action designed to achieve a particular goal.

   _____ is different from tactics. In military terms, tactics is concerned with the conduct of an engagement while _____ is concerned with how different engagements are linked.

   a. 180SearchAssistant
   b. Power III
   c. 6-3-5 Brainwriting
   d. Strategy

15. _____ is the pricing technique of setting a relatively low initial entry price, often lower than the eventual market price, to attract new customers. The strategy works on the expectation that customers will switch to the new brand because of the lower price. _____ is most commonly associated with a marketing objective of increasing market share or sales volume, rather than to make profit in the short term.

   a. Price war
   b. Penetration pricing
   c. Competitor indexing
   d. Fee

16. _____ is a pricing strategy in which a marketer sets a relatively high price for a product or service at first, then lowers the price over time. It is a temporal version of price discrimination/yield management. It allows the firm to recover its sunk costs quickly before competition steps in and lowers the market price.

   a. Relationship based pricing
   b. Price skimming
   c. Price markdown
   d. Discounts and allowances

Chapter 10. Pricing The Product

17. _____ are prices at which demand is relatively high. In introductory microeconomics, a demand curve is downward sloping to the right and either linear or gently convex to the origin. The first is usually true, but the second is only piecewise true, as price surveys indicate that demand for a product is not a linear function of its price and not even a smooth function.
   a. Price points
   b. Fee
   c. Price markdown
   d. Relationship based pricing

18. _____ or price ending is a marketing practice based on the theory that certain prices have a psychological impact. The retail prices are often expressed as 'odd prices': a little less than a round number, e.g. $19.99 or £6.95 (but not necessarily mathematically odd, it could also be 2.98.) The theory is this drives demand greater than would be expected if consumers were perfectly rational.
   a. First-mover advantage
   b. Psychological pricing
   c. Supplier diversity
   d. Chain stores

19. In economics, _____ are business expenses that are not dependent on the activities of the business They tend to be time-related, such as salaries or rents being paid per month. This is in contrast to variable costs, which are volume-related (and are paid per quantity.)

In management accounting, _____ are defined as expenses that do not change in proportion to the activity of a business, within the relevant period or scale of production.

   a. Fixed costs
   b. Marginal cost
   c. Transaction cost
   d. Variable cost

20. _____s are used in open sentences. For instance, in the formula $x + 1 = 5$, x is a _____ which represents an 'unknown' number. _____s are often represented by letters of the Roman alphabet, or those of other alphabets, such as Greek, and use other special symbols.
   a. Personalization
   b. Variable
   c. Book of business
   d. Quantitative

Chapter 10. Pricing The Product

21. _____s are expenses that change in proportion to the activity of a business. In other words, _____ is the sum of marginal costs. It can also be considered normal costs.

   a. Marginal cost
   b. Fixed costs
   c. Transaction cost
   d. Variable cost

22. In economics, business, retail, and accounting, a _____ is the value of money that has been used up to produce something, and hence is not available for use anymore. In economics, a _____ is an alternative that is given up as a result of a decision. In business, the _____ may be one of acquisition, in which case the amount of money expended to acquire it is counted as _____.

   a. Transaction cost
   b. Fixed costs
   c. Variable cost
   d. Cost

23. The break-even point for a product is the point where total revenue received equals the total costs associated with the sale of the product (TR=TC.) A break-even point is typically calculated in order for businesses to determine if it would be profitable to sell a proposed product, as opposed to attempting to modify an existing product instead so it can be made lucrative. _____ can also be used to analyse the potential profitability of an expenditure in a sales-based business.

   In _____, margin of safety is how much output or sales level can fall before a business reaches its break-even point (BEP).

   a. Contribution margin-based pricing
   b. Pay Per Sale
   c. Break even analysis
   d. Price skimming

24. _____, or Value optimized pricing is a business strategy. It sets selling prices on the perceived value to the customer, rather than on the actual cost of the product, the market price, competitors prices, or the historical price.

   The goal of _____ is to align price with value delivered.

   a. Jobbing house
   b. Money back guarantee
   c. Service-profit chain
   d. Value-based pricing

Chapter 10. Pricing The Product

25. _____ is a term used to describe a person who was born during the demographic Post-World War II baby boom. Many analysts now believe that two distinct cultural generations were born during this baby boom; the older generation is often called the Baby Boom Generation and the younger generation is often called Generation Jones. The term '_____' is sometimes used in a cultural context, and sometimes used to describe someone who was born during the post-WWII baby boom.
   a. AStore
   b. Greatest Generation
   c. Baby Boomer
   d. Generation X

26. _____ is an advertisement in which a particular product specifically mentions a competitor by name for the express purpose of showing why the competitor is inferior to the product naming it.

This should not be confused with parody advertisements, where a fictional product is being advertised for the purpose of poking fun at the particular advertisement, nor should it be confused with the use of a coined brand name for the purpose of comparing the product without actually naming an actual competitor. ('Wikipedia tastes better and is less filling than the Encyclopedia Galactica.')

In the 1980s, during what has been referred to as the cola wars, soft-drink manufacturer Pepsi ran a series of advertisements where people, caught on hidden camera, in a blind taste test, chose Pepsi over rival Coca-Cola.

   a. Heavy-up
   b. GL-70
   c. Comparative advertising
   d. Cost per conversion

Chapter 11. The Channels of Distribution

1. _____ generally refers to a list of all planned expenses and revenues. It is a plan for saving and spending. A _____ is an important concept in microeconomics, which uses a _____ line to illustrate the trade-offs between two or more goods.
   a. Power III
   b. Budget
   c. 6-3-5 Brainwriting
   d. 180SearchAssistant

2. _____ is defined by the American _____ Association as the activity, set of institutions, and processes for creating, communicating, delivering, and exchanging offerings that have value for customers, clients, partners, and society at large. The term developed from the original meaning which referred literally to going to market, as in shopping, or going to a market to sell goods or services.

   _____ practice tends to be seen as a creative industry, which includes advertising, distribution and selling.

   a. Customer acquisition management
   b. Marketing
   c. Product naming
   d. Marketing myopia

3. _____ can be regarded as an outcome of mental processes (cognitive process) leading to the selection of a course of action among several alternatives. Every _____ process produces a final choice. The output can be an action or an opinion of choice.
   a. 6-3-5 Brainwriting
   b. 180SearchAssistant
   c. Power III
   d. Decision making

4. _____ is a form of communication that typically attempts to persuade potential customers to purchase or to consume more of a particular brand of product or service. 'While now central to the contemporary global economy and the reproduction of global production networks, it is only quite recently that _____ has been more than a marginal influence on patterns of sales and production. The formation of modern _____ was intimately bound up with the emergence of new forms of monopoly capitalism around the end of the 19th and beginning of the 20th century as one element in corporate strategies to create, organize and where possible control markets, especially for mass produced consumer goods.
   a. AMAX
   b. Advertising
   c. ACNielsen
   d. ADTECH

Chapter 11. The Channels of Distribution

5. _____ is the state or fact of exclusive rights and control over property, which may be an object, land/real estate, or some other kind of property (like government-granted monopolies collectively referred to as intellectual property.) It is embodied in an _____ right also referred to as title.

_____ is the key building block in the development of the capitalist socio-economic system.

a. AMAX
b. Ownership
c. ACNielsen
d. ADTECH

6. _____ involves disseminating information about a product, product line, brand, or company. It is one of the four key aspects of the marketing mix. (The other three elements are product marketing, pricing, and distribution). P>_____ is generally sub-divided into two parts:

- Above the line _____: Promotion in the media (e.g. TV, radio, newspapers, Internet and Mobile Phones) in which the advertiser pays an advertising agency to place the ad
- Below the line _____: All other _____. Much of this is intended to be subtle enough for the consumer to be unaware that _____ is taking place. E.g. sponsorship, product placement, endorsements, sales _____, merchandising, direct mail, personal selling, public relations, trade shows

a. Cashmere Agency
b. Promotion
c. Davie Brown Index
d. Bottling lines

7. A _____ is a list of the general tasks and responsibilities of a position. Typically, it also includes to whom the position reports, specifications such as the qualifications needed by the person in the job, salary range for the position, etc. A _____ is usually developed by conducting a job analysis, which includes examining the tasks and sequences of tasks necessary to perform the job.
a. Power III
b. 6-3-5 Brainwriting
c. 180SearchAssistant
d. Job description

8. _____ consists of the sale of goods or merchandise from a fixed location, such as a department store or kiosk in small or individual lots for direct consumption by the purchaser. _____ may include subordinated services, such as delivery. Purchasers may be individuals or businesses.

a. Retailing
b. Warehouse store
c. Charity shop
d. Thrifting

9. _____ is one of the four elements of marketing mix. An organization or set of organizations (go-betweens) involved in the process of making a product or service available for use or consumption by a consumer or business user.

The other three parts of the marketing mix are product, pricing, and promotion.

a. Better Living Through Chemistry
b. Distribution
c. Japan Advertising Photographers' Association
d. Comparison-Shopping agent

10. _____, also referred to as i-marketing, web marketing, online marketing is the marketing of products or services over the Internet.

The Internet has brought many unique benefits to marketing, one of which being lower costs for the distribution of information and media to a global audience. The interactive nature of _____, both in terms of providing instant response and eliciting responses, is a unique quality of the medium.

a. ADTECH
b. AMAX
c. ACNielsen
d. Internet marketing

11. The business terms _____ and pull originated in the logistic and supply chain management, but are also widely used in marketing.

A _____-pull-system in business describes the move of a product or information between two subjects. On markets the consumers usually 'pulls' the goods or information they demand for their needs, while the offerers or suppliers '_____es' them toward the consumers.

a. Completely randomized designs
b. Gold Key Matching Service
c. Manufacturers' representatives
d. Push

12. _____ is a broad label that refers to any individuals or households that use goods and services generated within the economy. The concept of a _____ is used in different contexts, so that the usage and significance of the term may vary.

A _____ is a person who uses any product or service.

a. Consumer
b. Power III
c. 6-3-5 Brainwriting
d. 180SearchAssistant

13. A _____ is an explicit set of requirements to be satisfied by a material, product, or service.

In engineering, manufacturing, and business, it is vital for suppliers, purchasers, and users of materials, products, or services to understand and agree upon all requirements. A _____ is a type of a standard which is often referenced by a contract or procurement document.

a. Specification
b. Product optimization
c. New product development
d. Product development

Chapter 12. Raising Funds and Acquiring Volunteers

1. _____ is a fee paid on borrowed assets. It is the price paid for the use of borrowed money , or, money earned by deposited funds . Assets that are sometimes lent with _____ include money, shares, consumer goods through hire purchase, major assets such as aircraft, and even entire factories in finance lease arrangements.

   a. ACNielsen
   b. Interest
   c. AMAX
   d. ADTECH

2. _____ is one of the four Ps of the marketing mix. The other three aspects are product, promotion, and place. It is also a key variable in microeconomic price allocation theory.

   a. Competitor indexing
   b. Relationship based pricing
   c. Pricing
   d. Price

3. _____ or _____ data refers to selected population characteristics as used in government, marketing or opinion research, or the _____ profiles used in such research. Note the distinction from the term 'demography' Commonly-used _____ include race, age, income, disabilities, mobility (in terms of travel time to work or number of vehicles available), educational attainment, home ownership, employment status, and even location.

   a. AStore
   b. Demographic
   c. Albert Einstein
   d. African Americans

4. The _____ is a model used to represent the process of explaining the transformation of countries from high birth rates and high death rates to low birth rates and low death rates as part of the economic development of a country from a pre-industrial to an industrialized economy. It is based on an interpretation begun in 1929 by the American demographer Warren Thompson of prior observed changes, or transitions, in birth and death rates in industrialized societies over the past two hundred years.

Most developed countries are beyond stage three of the model; the majority of developing countries are in stage 2 or stage 3.

   a. 6-3-5 Brainwriting
   b. Power III
   c. 180SearchAssistant
   d. Demographic transition model

Chapter 12. Raising Funds and Acquiring Volunteers

5. _____ is the study of the Earth and its lands, features, inhabitants, and phenomena. A literal translation would be 'to describe or write about the Earth'. The first person to use the word '_____' was Eratosthenes .
   a. 180SearchAssistant
   b. Power III
   c. Geography
   d. 6-3-5 Brainwriting

6. _____ is systematic determination of merit, worth, and significance of something or someone using criteria against a set of standards. _____ often is used to characterize and appraise subjects of interest in a wide range of human enterprises, including the arts, criminal justice, foundations and non-profit organizations, government, health care, and other human services.

Depending on the topic of interest, there are professional groups which look to the quality and rigor of the _____ process.

   a. ADTECH
   b. AMAX
   c. ACNielsen
   d. Evaluation

7. _____ can be regarded as an outcome of mental processes (cognitive process) leading to the selection of a course of action among several alternatives. Every _____ process produces a final choice. The output can be an action or an opinion of choice.
   a. Power III
   b. 6-3-5 Brainwriting
   c. 180SearchAssistant
   d. Decision making

8. _____ is a broad label that refers to any individuals or households that use goods and services generated within the economy. The concept of a _____ is used in different contexts, so that the usage and significance of the term may vary.

A _____ is a person who uses any product or service.

   a. 6-3-5 Brainwriting
   b. Power III
   c. 180SearchAssistant
   d. Consumer

Chapter 12. Raising Funds and Acquiring Volunteers

9. Advertising mail junk mail is the delivery of advertising material to recipients of postal mail. The delivery of advertising mail forms a large and growing service for many postal services, and _____ marketing forms a significant portion of the direct marketing industry. Some organizations attempt to help people opt-out of receiving advertising mail, in many cases motivated by a concern over its negative environmental impact.

   a. Telemarketing
   b. Phishing
   c. Direct mail
   d. Directory Harvest Attack

10. _____ is defined by the American _____ Association as the activity, set of institutions, and processes for creating, communicating, delivering, and exchanging offerings that have value for customers, clients, partners, and society at large. The term developed from the original meaning which referred literally to going to market, as in shopping, or going to a market to sell goods or services.

   _____ practice tends to be seen as a creative industry, which includes advertising, distribution and selling.

   a. Marketing
   b. Product naming
   c. Marketing myopia
   d. Customer acquisition management

11. A _____ is a body of elected or appointed persons who jointly oversee the activities of a company or organization. The body sometimes has a different name, such as board of trustees, board of governors, board of managers, or executive board. It is often simply referred to as 'the board.'

   A board's activities are determined by the powers, duties, and responsibilities delegated to it or conferred on it by an authority outside itself.

   a. Board of directors
   b. Colour trademark
   c. Comparative negligence
   d. Federal Food, Drug, and Cosmetic Act

12. A _____ is the price one pays as remuneration for services, especially the honorarium paid to a doctor, lawyer, consultant, or other member of a learned profession. _____s usually allow for overhead, wages, costs, and markup.

   Traditionally, professionals in Great Britain received a _____ in contradistinction to a payment, salary, or wage, and would often use guineas rather than pounds as units of account.

Chapter 12. Raising Funds and Acquiring Volunteers

a. Transfer pricing
b. Price shading
c. Price war
d. Fee

13. In the mathematical discipline of graph theory a _____ or edge-independent set in a graph is a set of edges without common vertices. It may also be an entire graph consisting of edges without common vertices.

Given a graph G = (V,E), a _____ M in G is a set of pairwise non-adjacent edges; that is, no two edges share a common vertex.

a. 180SearchAssistant
b. Power III
c. 6-3-5 Brainwriting
d. Matching

14. _____ is an advertisement in which a particular product specifically mentions a competitor by name for the express purpose of showing why the competitor is inferior to the product naming it.

This should not be confused with parody advertisements, where a fictional product is being advertised for the purpose of poking fun at the particular advertisement, nor should it be confused with the use of a coined brand name for the purpose of comparing the product without actually naming an actual competitor. ('Wikipedia tastes better and is less filling than the Encyclopedia Galactica.')

In the 1980s, during what has been referred to as the cola wars, soft-drink manufacturer Pepsi ran a series of advertisements where people, caught on hidden camera, in a blind taste test, chose Pepsi over rival Coca-Cola.

a. Comparative advertising
b. GL-70
c. Cost per conversion
d. Heavy-up

15. _____ is a method of direct marketing in which a salesperson solicits to prospective customers to buy products or services, either over the phone or through a subsequent face to face or Web conferencing appointment scheduled during the call.

_____ can also include recorded sales pitches programmed to be played over the phone via automatic dialing. _____ has come under fire in recent years, being viewed as an annoyance by many.

Chapter 12. Raising Funds and Acquiring Volunteers

a. Phishing
b. Directory Harvest Attack
c. Joe job
d. Telemarketing

16. _____ generally refers to a list of all planned expenses and revenues. It is a plan for saving and spending. A _____ is an important concept in microeconomics, which uses a _____ line to illustrate the trade-offs between two or more goods.
    a. Power III
    b. 6-3-5 Brainwriting
    c. 180SearchAssistant
    d. Budget

17. _____ is the set of reasons that determines one to engage in a particular behavior. The term is generally used for human _____ but, theoretically, it can be used to describe the causes for animal behavior as well
    a. Power III
    b. Role playing
    c. 180SearchAssistant
    d. Motivation

ANSWER KEY

Chapter 1
1. b   2. a   3. b   4. c   5. a   6. d   7. d   8. c   9. d   10. b
11. d   12. d   13. b

Chapter 2
1. d   2. d   3. b   4. d   5. d   6. d   7. b   8. b   9. b   10. b
11. c   12. d   13. d   14. d   15. d   16. c   17. c   18. d   19. d   20. d
21. d   22. d   23. d   24. c   25. c   26. c   27. b   28. d   29. b   30. d
31. b   32. b   33. d   34. d   35. d   36. d

Chapter 3
1. d   2. a   3. b   4. d   5. b   6. a   7. c   8. d   9. b   10. a
11. a   12. c   13. a   14. d   15. c   16. c   17. d   18. d   19. d   20. d
21. d   22. a   23. d

Chapter 4
1. d   2. a   3. d   4. b   5. b   6. d   7. c   8. a   9. d   10. c
11. d   12. d   13. a   14. d   15. a   16. d   17. d   18. a   19. d   20. d
21. d

Chapter 5
1. b   2. d   3. a   4. d   5. d   6. d   7. d   8. a   9. a   10. c
11. d   12. d   13. c   14. d   15. a   16. a   17. d   18. c   19. d   20. c
21. b   22. d   23. d   24. d   25. b   26. d   27. d   28. d   29. d   30. a

Chapter 6
1. b   2. d   3. a   4. c   5. c   6. b   7. d   8. d   9. c   10. d
11. c   12. c   13. a   14. d   15. c   16. d

Chapter 7
1. b   2. b   3. d   4. d   5. d   6. c   7. d   8. b   9. d   10. a
11. d   12. b   13. d   14. b   15. d   16. d   17. d   18. d   19. a   20. d
21. d   22. d   23. c

Chapter 8
1. d   2. b   3. d   4. b   5. a   6. d   7. b   8. a   9. b   10. c
11. c   12. d   13. d   14. d   15. d   16. d   17. d   18. b   19. d   20. d
21. a   22. d   23. d   24. c   25. d   26. d   27. d   28. d   29. b   30. b
31. d   32. d   33. c   34. c   35. a   36. b   37. d   38. d

Chapter 9
1. d   2. d   3. c   4. d   5. d   6. a   7. b   8. d   9. a   10. b
11. d   12. c   13. d   14. d   15. b   16. b   17. d   18. b   19. d   20. b
21. a   22. d   23. d   24. b

Chapter 10

1. d	2. d	3. d	4. d	5. d	6. d	7. a	8. c	9. d	10. d
11. b	12. c	13. d	14. d	15. b	16. b	17. a	18. b	19. a	20. b
21. d	22. d	23. c	24. d	25. c	26. c				

Chapter 11

| 1. b | 2. b | 3. d | 4. b | 5. b | 6. b | 7. d | 8. a | 9. b | 10. d |
| 11. d | 12. a | 13. a | | | | | | | |

Chapter 12

| 1. b | 2. c | 3. b | 4. d | 5. c | 6. d | 7. d | 8. d | 9. c | 10. a |
| 11. a | 12. d | 13. d | 14. a | 15. d | 16. d | 17. d | | | |

www.ingramcontent.com/pod-product-compliance
Lightning Source LLC
Chambersburg PA
CBHW081847230426
43669CB00018B/2850